Homosexuality

ISSUES
(previously Issues for the Nineties)

Volume 23

Editor

Craig Donnellan

Independence

First published by Independence
PO Box 295
Cambridge CB1 3XP
England

© Craig Donnellan 1998

British Library Cataloguing in Publication Data
Homosexuality– (Issues Series)
I. Donnellan, Craig II. Series
306.7'66

ISBN 1 86168 055 4

Printed in Great Britain
City Print Ltd
Milton Keynes

Typeset by
Claire Boyd

Cover
The illustration on the front cover is by
The Attic Publishing Co.

CONTENTS

Introduction

Homosexuality is the twenty-third volume in the series: **Issues**. The aim of this series is to offer up-to-date information about important issues in our world.

Homosexuality looks at the legal, social and moral aspects of gay and lesbian relationships.

The information comes from a wide variety of sources and includes:
Government reports and statistics
Newspaper reports and features
Magazine articles and surveys
Literature from lobby groups
and charitable organisations.

It is hoped that, as you read about the many aspects of the issues explored in this book, you will critically evaluate the information presented. It is important that you decide whether you are being presented with facts or opinions. Does the writer give a biased or an unbiased report? If an opinion is being expressed, do you agree with the writer?

Homosexuality offers a useful starting-point for those who need convenient access to information about the many issues involved. However, it is only a starting-point. At the back of the book is a list of organisations which you may want to contact for further information.

*****

Gay sex and the law

Information from Stonewall

How the law criminalises gay sex

Gay sex was partially decriminalised in 1967 but it is still basically illegal, subject to an exception for consenting adults in private. The law breaks gay sex down to two offences: 'buggery' (which can also be a heterosexual offence) and 'gross indecency between males', which is any gay sex other than anal intercourse. These acts are treated as offences in themselves, whereas heterosexual sex is basically lawful unless there is something which makes it unlawful, e.g. unlawful sexual intercourse with a girl under 16.

The Sexual Offences Act 1967 decriminalised gay sex between consenting adults in private in England and Wales, but not in the armed forces or the merchant navy.

Gay sex remained completely illegal until 1981 in Scotland and 1982 in Northern Ireland. It ceased to be a criminal offence in the armed forces and the merchant navy in 1994.

The age of consent

The age of consent for gay sex was reduced from 21 to 18 in 1994. This still discriminated against gay men because the age of consent for heterosexuals is 16.

The number of prosecutions is low but when they do come to court age of consent offences are taken very seriously and prison sentences are still imposed.

Young gay men are themselves committing an offence if they have sex before they are 18. By contrast a girl under 16 commits no offence if she has sexual intercourse whilst under age – only her partner does.

Although young men under 18 are rarely prosecuted, the law sends out a signal to young gay men that if they have sex they are doing something wrong.

The privacy requirement

The 1967 Act imposed a very restrictive definition of privacy which gay sex must meet before it is lawful. This means that gay sex is always unlawful if it takes place outside a private dwelling, and even in your own home it is unlawful if more than two people are present. Heterosexual sex is never an offence in itself – and it is only a minor offence at common law if it takes place in public. The same goes for lesbian sex.

Prosecutions

In 1995 there were nearly 500 prosecutions for gross indecency. Nearly 90% of these involved sex in public rather than age of consent offences. However all of those people are tainted with a criminal record for an offence which could relate to child abuse.

Of the 10% relating to age of consent offences, we believe most if not all of these relate to sex with 16 and 17-year-olds, i.e. acts which would not even be an offence if they

involved sex with a girl of that age instead of a boy. One in four of these convictions resulted in sentences of immediate custody.

The age of consent for lesbian sex

Lesbian sex has never been illegal in Britain. An attempt to criminalise it in 1921 was successful in the House of Commons but was rejected by the House of Lords, where opponents pointed out that to do so might 'bring it to the notice of women who have never heard of it'!

It is not true however that there is no age of consent for lesbian sex – there is, and it is 16. Lesbian sex is not explicitly mentioned in the law, but a girl of under 16 is deemed not capable of consenting to any sexual act. Under-age lesbian sex can be (and has been) prosecuted as 'indecent assault on a girl under 16'. This carries a penalty of up to 10 years.

The campaign for equality

In 1993 Stonewall sponsored three young men – Ralph Wilde, Hugo Greenhalgh and Will Parry – to take the government to court under the European Convention on Human Rights. This together with the lobbying to the Home Office led to the government agreeing to make time available for a debate and a free vote on the age of consent in early 1994.

The proposal for an equal age of consent was sponsored by MPs Edwina Currie, Neil Kinnock and Robert Maclennan. In the weeks before the debate there was one of the biggest lobbies ever organised. MPs received thousands of letters from lesbians and gay men, and there was a broad public debate about the positions of lesbians and gay men in society.

The vote for equality was lost by only 27 votes – 307 votes to 280. The vote for 18 was passed by an overwhelming majority. 39 Labour voted against 16; 44 Conservatives voted for 16. All but one Liberal Democrat voted for 16.

The then Home Secretary, Michael Howard, argued against equality saying that homosexuals are still set apart from society and young

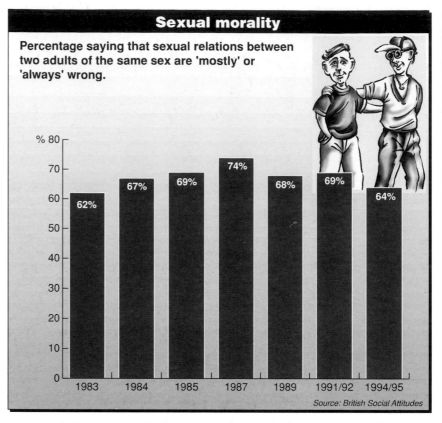

Sexual morality

Percentage saying that sexual relations between two adults of the same sex are 'mostly' or 'always' wrong.

Source: British Social Attitudes

men must be protected from an unhappy lifestyle.

Tony Blair, then Shadow Home Secretary, argued for an equal age of consent, saying 'the most basic civilised value is the notion of respect for other people . . . that it why it is wrong to treat a man as inferior because his sexuality is different'.

European comparisons

There is now an equal age of consent in 12 out of 15 countries in the EC: Belgium (16), Denmark (15), France (15), Germany (16), the Netherlands (16), Portugal (16), Spain (12), and Sweden (15).

All of these countries have managed to equalise their age of consent without encountering any of the problems predicted by opponents of equality in this country.

Besides the UK, there is still an unequal age of consent in Austria (14/18) and Finland (16/18 for gay sex and for lesbian sex).

The European test cases

Stonewall argues that the unequal age of consent is a breach of the European Convention on Human Rights. Article 8 of the Convention say everyone is entitled to respect for their private life and family life; article 14 provides that there should

be no discrimination in the enjoyment of the rights set out in the convention.

The case involving Ralph Wilde, Hugo Greenhalgh and Will Parry was declared not admissible after the age of consent was reduced to 18, because all three were aged over 18 when they took the case. However, Stonewall immediately launched another case, involving Euan Sutherland, who was 17 at the time. A similar case involving another 17-year-old, Chris Morris, was brought two years later, to keep the same momentum going.

Euan's application reached the European Commission on Human Rights in May 1996. Euan's lawyers argued that it is sex discrimination that there is a different age for gays and for heterosexuals, and that it is wrong that a law which purports to protect young people actually criminalises them.

The Commission decide there was a prima facie breach of the Convention. This was the first time in seven such cases that the Commission found for the applicant. In principle the case should now go to a full hearing of the European Court of Human Rights some time in 1998. However to avoid this happening the new government have now agreed to allow a free vote on the age of consent during the 1997-98 session of Parliament.

It is not yet known when this will be – probably around spring 1998. Nor is it known how exactly the vote will take place. It could be a vote on an amendment to a government bill, in which case if passed it could become law by autumn 1998. If this is not possible there will be a vote on a resolution, and if the resolution is carried, there will be government legislation to implement it in the 1998-9 session of Parliament.

How the law should be reformed

Another question that remains to be decided is how the amendment for equality will be framed. If the existing legal structure which defines gay sex as 'gross indecency' and 'buggery' is retained, then the criminal law will remain grossly discriminatory against gay men.

Only 10% of convictions for gross indecency between men represent age of consent offences. The others involve sex in public, and the men charged with these offences will still face overzealous policing, unduly harsh charges and unfair penalities if only the age of consent is changed.

For example, a heterosexual couple making love in a public park or a parked car or a doorway could in theory be charged with 'outraging public decency'. But such prosecutions are very rare, and the penalties are much lower. By way of comparison, in 1994, 28 men were convicted of gross indecency for offences which only came to light because of police undercover operations in a public toilet, and were fined £250 each. By contrast in 1992 a heterosexual couple who had intercourse on a train in full view of other passengers were fined just £25 each.

It is not just that the penalties for gay sex are much harsher. There is enormous stigma attached to a conviction for gross indecency, partly because the public perceives it to be a much more serious offence than it really is (58% of heterosexuals in a recent survey thought it might mean flashing in a school playground, and 28% thought it might mean raping a child), and partly because it could relate to under-age sex. Men convicted of gross indecency often lose their jobs as a result, and case law suggests that they would lose any claim for unfair dismissal. Even a caution for gross indecency will show on police checks and can end the career of anyone working in teaching, youth work or the caring professions.

We believe that the law should not confuse sex in public with sex with children. Everyone should be subject to the same charges for the same kind of offence; the same penalties should attach to those charges; and the law should be enforced equally against heterosexuals and homosexuals alike.

This could be achieved at the same time as equalising the age of consent. 'Gross indecency' could be repealed altogether – it is quite unnecessary. Sex with a boy under 16 would still be unlawful because a young person under 16 cannot in law consent to any sexual activity; even if they do consent, the older person commits an indecent assault.

Public sex offences could either be dealt with under the common law (like heterosexual sex), or could be dealt with as a minor public order offence which would apply equally to heterosexuals, lesbians and gay men.

© Stonewall
March, 1998

Age of consent

		Male/Female	Female/Female	Male/Male	Equal since
	Belgium	16	16	16	1985
	Finland	16	18	18	-
	France	15	15	15	1982
	Germany	16	16	16	1994
	Greece	15	15	15	1987
	Iceland	14	14	14	1992
	Ireland[1]	17	15	17	1993
	Italy	16	16	16	1889
	Lithuania[2]	14	-	-	-
	Malta	12	12	12	1973
	San Marino	14	14	14	1865
	Slovenia	14	14	14	1977
	Spain	12	12	12	1822
	Sweden	15	15	15	1978
	Turkey[3]	15/18	15/18	15/18	-
	UK	16	16	18	-

1 In Ireland, the age of consent for intercourse is 17, except in the case of heterosexual couples who may marry at 16 with their parents' consent. The age of consent for other sex acts is 15 for heterosexuals and lesbians and 17 for gay men.
2 Lithuania has no legislation on the age of consent for gay sex acts.
3 Turkey allows penetrative vaginal and anal sex at 18 and other sex acts at 15, regardless of gender or sexual orientation.

A global map of discrimination

In many countries homosexuality remains a criminal offence, often punishable by lengthy prison sentences or, in some cases, execution

The global map of discrimination is designed to give a brief outline of the legal and social position of lesbians and gay men in a range of countries where War On Want has an interest. We have tried not to assume that all persecution is legal in nature. In some countries that have no sodomy laws, or where laws have been repealed, you may find instances of persecution carried out directly by the state in the form of 'hooliganism laws' or 'decency' laws, or in the selective persecution of lesbians and gays under other laws. Or persecution may be carried out by non-state agents while the state is unwilling or unable to control them. This is particularly true in cases of lesbian persecution, since very few countries have sodomy laws that directly penalise same gender sexual relations between women.

It is also worth remembering that we cannot assume a common identity as lesbian or gay in other cultures, similar to our own more common western understanding. What we can assume is that where law suggests or reports show persecution because of sexual orientation, that there are individuals or communities that deserve our support and help.

Mexico

The situation in Mexico is quite complex. On the one hand, Mexico boasts a large number of gay organisations, some of them quite old and well established. On the other hand, there are many instances of discrimination and persecution, such as murders of gay men and transvestites in the states of Chiapas and Sinaloa, and reports of police repression against gay men and transvestites in the city of Chihuahua in 1995 and the killing of activists in Mexico City.

Nicaragua

In March 94 the Nicaraguan Supreme Court upheld legislation introduced in 1992 to penalise homosexuality. Article 204 provides that 'anyone who induces, promotes, propagandises or practices in scandalous form sexual intercourse between persons of the same sex commits the crime of sodomy'. The article also contains a provision criminalising homosexual relations in private where one of the partners is in a position of responsibility over the other. The law also permits the persecution of individuals for activities such as advocating lesbian and gay rights, imparting health information about sexuality, or having homosexual relations in circumstances which are not criminal if they involve heterosexuals.

Jamaica

Homosexual behaviour is illegal making homosexual intercourse between men a crime, punishable with imprisonment and hard labour for up to ten years.

Iran

In Iran the Sharia (Islamic law) is applied. Homosexuality is considered 'one of the worst possible sins imaginable' which has to be punished

severely, and the Islamic Penal Code allows for prison sentences, whipping, chopping off of hands and feet, stoning and sentences of death. The execution of homosexuals has been reported. It is not necessary that a complaint be put to the authorities; a judge is allowed to take action by himself.

Libya

Sharia, the Islamic law, which punishes homosexual acts, is enforced severely with imprisonment for homosexual acts of between three and five years.

Ecuador

Homosexual acts can be punished with up to eight years' imprisonment, eight years for the 'aggressor' in cases of force or violence, four to eight years for both parties in the case of consenting adults. Homosexuals are often subjected to police harassment and violence. In 1993, twenty gay men were killed by death squads.

Pakistan

Laws prohibit 'carnal intercourse against the order of nature with any man', with a punishment of two years to life imprisonment, which may be extended to include corporal punishment of 100 lashes. Homosexuality is taboo. When homosexual acts become known, the people involved will become social outcasts.

India

Homosexual acts between men are illegal. The Penal Code criminalises 'carnal intercourse against the order of nature with man, woman or animal' with a maximum penalty of life imprisonment. There are reports of raids by the police in Bombay, with homosexuals being arrested for no other reason than that they 'look like' homosexuals.

China

Homosexuality is considered to be a 'foreigners' disease'. Homosexual behaviour between consenting adults is not mentioned in the law as being a criminal offence. There are, however, reports of homosexuals being imprisoned on specious grounds, such as section 158 of the penal code, which penalises 'disturbance against the social order' with up to five years in jail. All visitors from Hong Kong, Taiwan, and Macau now have to present a certificate of HIV-negativity before they can enter the country, and reports exist of homosexuals being subjected to electric shock 'therapy' to cure them. In April 1992 the Chinese Ministry of Public Security concluded that there were no legal reasons to separate lesbians who were living together. Homosexual men have fled the country and have been accepted as political refugees on the grounds of fear of persecution because of their sexual preference in a small number of countries.

Chile

Male homosexual acts are illegal. Article 165 of the Penal Code sanctions consenting male homosexual activity as a sodomy delict with a penalty of one and a half to three years' imprisonment. The penalty depends on the complaints of the 'victim'. Lesbian sexual contacts are not mentioned in the law. Homosexuals are often subjected to official and police harassment and violence. A policy exists of compulsory HIV testing of all known gay men. Gay and lesbian groups exist but are illegal. In Santiago a lesbian group which set up in 1987 received death threats from right-wing groups.

Ethiopia

Homosexual acts between men and between women are illegal with a penalty of 'simple imprisonment' from ten days to three years, with the possibility of increasing the penalty with five years or more. This depends on whether the offender takes advantage of the position of authority in order to exercise influence over the other person, or whether the offender 'makes a profession of such activities'.

Brazil

Although Brazil has strong lesbian and gay rights movement, it also has some of the worst examples of oppression of lesbians and gays in the world. Although homosexuality is not illegal, the police use the pretext of 'safeguarding morality and public decency' and 'preventing outrageous behaviour' to stop, arrest, and bring homosexuals to trial, whereas they would not bother heterosexuals in similar situations. Several cities have adopted anti-discrimination regulations which protect homosexuals. A minority of the population is in favour of lesbian and gay rights. There are, however, reports of more than 320 lesbians and gays being killed in the Bahia in the recent past because of their sexual orientation.

Algeria

Homosexual acts between men and between women are illegal according to section 338 of the penal code with a maximum penalty of three years' imprisonment. Openly homosexual relationships are not possible and homosexuality cannot be discussed in public.

Ghana

Homosexual behaviour is illegal. Article 303a of the Penal Code of April 30 1988, sanctions it as a 'public scandal' with three months to one year of imprisonment, or a fine for 'people persistently bothering others with homosexual amorous advances'. Homosexuals are often subjected to official police harassment and violence. In 1992 there were reports of torture and imprisonment of gay men.

Zimbabwe

Homosexual behaviour between males is a criminal offence. The President of Zimbabwe, Robert Mugabe, has led a virulent attack on the country's lesbians and gays stating that activism in support of homosexual emancipation will not be tolerated. Mugabe's government has a history of harassing lesbians and gays. In the past he has called homosexuality 'a white problem' and government officials have threatened to arrest gays and lesbians.

Bangladesh

Homosexual behaviour is illegal; Islamic laws against homosexuality are applied. The government's official stance is that homosexuality does not exist. Socially, homosexuality is considered to be a perversion.

Argentina

Although homosexual behaviour between consenting adults is not mentioned in the law as being a criminal offence, many provinces have 'edictos policiales' on the basis of which one can be detained for 30 days for 'offences against morality' and for 48 hours for 'documentation controls'. These rules are used especially against gay men and make registration of them possible. Homosexuality is hardly discussed or seen in public and society is strongly influenced by a conservative, anti-homosexual Catholic church.

Singapore

Homosexual behaviour, both male and female, is illegal. The law punishes 'carnal intercourse against the order of nature' with ten years' to life imprisonment.

Malaysia

Homosexual behaviour is illegal. Laws punish whoever voluntarily has 'carnal intercourse against the order of nature with any man, woman or animal,' with a maximum penalty of twenty years' imprisonment and a fine of whipping.

• The above information is by War on Want. See page 41 for address details.

© War on Want

Same-sex couples and the law

Information from Stonewall

Discrimination against same-sex couples

Lesbian and gay couples face discrimination in three ways:

1) legally, same-sex couples are not allowed to marry;

2) legally, same-sex couples living together are not recognised even in circumstances where an unmarried heterosexual couple would be recognised as 'living together as man and wife'; and

3) there is no law against employers, hotel owners and other service providers discriminating against same-sex couples if they choose to.

Discrimination by employers, hotels etc.

Equal pay

Many employers provide benefits in respect of a husband or wife or (in some cases) a heterosexual partner, but refuse to provide the same benefits to same-sex partners. The best known example is South West Trains, which provides a free travel pass to heterosexual partners of employees but not to same-sex partners. Other examples include health insurance, life insurance, cheap or free use of the employer's services, and pensions.

Many pension schemes provide dependant's pensions only for a widow or widower. In these schemes a gay or lesbian partner can never benefit no matter how long they lived together. Some schemes provide a pension only to a heterosexual dependant. The Inland Revenue recently made it clear that it does not object to same-sex partners receiving a dependant's pensions; but pension schemes are not obliged to stop discriminating.

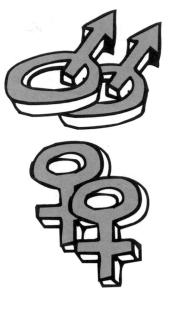

Discrimination in the provision of services

Most hotels do not discriminate against same-sex couples, but a significant minority do. The *Independent on Sunday* recently tried to book a double room for a same-sex couple at ten hotels featured in the *Which?* guide. Three refused a booking for a same-sex couple. Many insurers also discriminate against same-sex couples or in some cases against unmarried couples.

Rights of cohabiting straight couples

In housing law

Married and unmarried heterosexual couples have the right to succeed to a council tenancy, housing association tenancy or Rent Act tenancy. Lesbian and gay couples do not.

In the mental health field

Under the Mental Health Act a heterosexual partner of only six months is recognised as a person's 'nearest relative'; a gay partner is only recognised if they have lived together for five years and the person

who is mentally ill has no living relatives in this country. This means same-sex partners have no right to be consulted if their partner is subject to compulsory detention or to apply for their discharge.

In other areas

Couples 'living together as man and wife' are also recognised in other laws for example the Inheritance (Provision for Families and Dependants) Act 1975 and the Fatal Accidents Compensation Act 1976.

In social security

Cohabiting same-sex couples benefit from not being recognised, because they are treated as individuals whereas heterosexual couples are assumed to provide for each other.

Rights of married couples

Tax perks

Married couples can leave as much property as they like to each other in their will – no matter how big their estate, their widow or widower will not have to pay inheritance tax. Same-sex couples cannot do this. After the first £223,000 they pay tax at 40%. Married couples also benefit from the married couple's tax allowance – currently worth £285 a year (£500 to couples aged over 65). Married couples can also transfer as much property as they like from one to the other without becoming liable for Capital Gains Tax.

Inheritance provision on intestacy

When a person dies without leaving a will, their property goes to their spouse, their children or their blood relatives but it cannot go to an unmarried partner. Two out of three people have not made a will, but most heterosexuals are married so their property would go to their partner. Lesbians and gay men can be thrown out of their home by their partner's family if their partner dies without leaving a will.

Immigration

Gay men and lesbians whose partner comes from outside the European Union have no right in law to have their partner come and live with them in Britain. Under a concession introduced by the Labour government, same-sex partners can now come here if the couple have lived together for four years – but this can be hard to achieve if there is nowhere where both of them can live! Married couples by contrast get one year's leave to remain immediately they marry, and the right to residency follows at the end of that year.

Adoption

Unmarried couples are not allowed to adopt jointly. This makes it difficult for same-sex couples to adopt. Where they do succeed in adopting, only one of them becomes the legal parent.

If the relationship ends

When a couple marry they undertake to care for and provide for each other. If they split up the courts will adjudicate as to property and in some cases maintenance. Same-sex couples are legally barred from making this sort of commitment to each other.

Legal reforms needed

A law against discrimination

It is now unlawful to discriminate on grounds of sex, race or disability in the employment field or in the provision of goods and services. Lesbians and gay men should have the same protection under the law. It should be unlawful for employers to discriminate against lesbian and gay employees by providing pensions or other benefits for married or heterosexual partners but not for same-sex partners. Equally it should be unlawful for hotels, landlords or local authorities to discriminate against same-sex couples.

The Sexual Orientation Discrimination Bill would make such discrimination unlawful by amending the Sex Discrimination Act.

Stonewall hopes to see the Bill tabled soon in the House of Lords, and towards the end of the year in the House of Commons. If it is not successful, we would also hope that the government would legislate against such discrimination when it next amends the Sex Discrimination Act.

Recognition for cohabiting couples

Every law that currently refers to couples 'living together as man and wife' should be amended to recognise any two people 'living together as a couple'.

The law should recognise cohabiting couples in other situations too. Many of the rights currently given only to married couples should be extended to unmarried couples in committed long-term relationships. For example, in immigration law, the test should be whether there is a genuine long-term relationship, not whether the couple have gone through a marriage ceremony. All relationships should be subject to the same scrutiny, and no one should have to wait four years to be with their loved one.

Similarly, the marriage requirement for joint adoption by couples should be removed – couples should be assessed on the basis of the strength of their relationship, not whether they can show a marriage certificate.

Some privileges for married couples, for example the married couple's tax allowance, could simply be phased out– there is no justification for it.

In some areas however it would be difficult to legislate to recognise cohabiting couples. For example, the Law Commission recommended against allowing cohabitees to inherit their partner's property if their partner died intestate, because it said this would lead to a large number of claims which would need to be assessed, leading to increased costs and delays in the administration of estates. It is likely to remain the case that unmarried partners must make a will if they wish their partner to inherit their property.

Law reform is also needed to regulate the property rights of cohabiting couples when their relationship breaks down. The Law Commission is currently considering this. Many heterosexual couples wrongly believe that they are living in a 'common law marriage' – in fact there is no such thing. In Australia, a number of states impose financial responsibilities on couples who have lived together for two years or more,

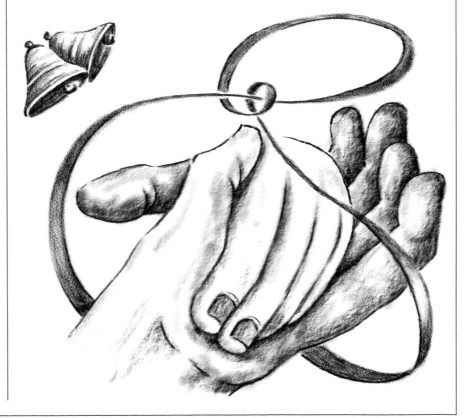

or who have children together, unless they contract out of these responsibilities. If such a reform is introduced here, it should also apply to same-sex couples.

A partnership law?
Registered partnership laws have now been passed in Denmark (1989), Sweden (1995), Iceland (1996), Greenland (1996), and the Netherlands (1997). In these countries a registered partnership is almost – but not quite – the same as a civil marriage. The differences are: that it is called partnership instead of marriage, that you cannot register your partnership in church, that one partner must be a citizen of one of the above countries (so a British couple cannot just go to Denmark to register their partnership), that the partnerships are designed to take effect only in that country (whereas marriage is valid anywhere in the world), and finally that the right to joint custody or joint adoption of

children is expressly excluded. (The Greenland law does allow a couple to apply for joint custody of their own children, and the Dutch law allows same-sex couples to adopt Dutch children, but not children from overseas.)

In all of these countries except the Netherlands, partnership is a separate institution for same-sex couples only, which tends to ghettoise lesbians and gay men. Lesbians and gay men are still excluded from marriage, so there is still discrimination and there are still lesbians and gay men who are not satisfied with partnership laws for this reason. In the Netherlands, there is still a campaign for the right to marry despite the recent enactment of a partnership law.

The right to marry
In the USA lesbians and gay men have been campaigning for the right to marry rather than a partnership law. In 1993 the Hawaii Supreme Court ruled that three same-sex couples should be allowed favour to marry. A ban on same-sex marriages was sex discrimination just as a ban on mixed-race marriages would be race discrimination; as such it was unconstitutional. This ruling was appealed and a final decision is now awaited. If same-sex marriage becomes legal in Hawaii, couples from all over the world (including the UK) will fly to Hawaii, get married, and then seek legal recognition for their marriage in their home country – whether in the context of immigration, pension rights, inheritance or even divorce.

Lisa Grant and Jill Percey lost their case in the European Court of Justice partly on the basis that they were not married. The marriage bar underpins discrimination against same-sex couples; sooner or later we will have to fight to end it.

© Stonewall
March, 1998

Breaking the silence

Sexual minorities at risk

In countries all over the world, individuals are being targeted for imprisonment, torture and even murder, simply on the grounds of their sexual orientation. Gay men, lesbians, transvestites, transsexuals – any person who doesn't adhere to the dictates of what passes for 'normal' sexuality – may be subject to such persecution at the hands of private individuals or government agents. Abuses may take subtle forms such as everyday hostility, harassment or neglect. In such cases, antipathetic authorities may refuse to protect the basic rights of gays and lesbians, leaving them vulnerable to exploitation, sexual attack, public or domestic violence and even murder, all without recourse to the law. In other instances, governments are themselves the perpetrators of

abuses: unfair trials, imprisonment, ill-treatment (including false 'medical cures'), torture (including rape), and execution are among the violations recorded by Amnesty International.

No international protection for sexual minorities
Much of the impetus for the development of international human rights law as it exists today emerged in reaction to the atrocities committed during the Second World War. Like Jews, gypsies, and the disabled, lesbians and gay men were targeted for extermination by the Nazis. As many as one hundred thousand men were identified as homosexuals and transported to concentration camps. Wearing the pink triangle (since adopted as the international symbol

of the gay rights movement), these men were among the millions shot, hanged, gassed, worked or starved to death in the camps. Thousands of lesbians met the same fate. Identified not as homosexuals but as 'anti-social elements', lesbians wore the black triangle and lived, laboured, starved and died alongside vagrants and petty criminals who had received the same classification.

Despite this clear indication of their particular vulnerability to human rights abuses, gay men and lesbians were not specifically included in the framework for international human rights protection when the United Nations drew up the Universal Declaration of Human Rights after the war's end. Systematic discrimination against some vulnerable groups has been addressed in subsequent documents such as the International Covenant on the Elimination of All Forms of Racial Discrimination and the International Covenant on the Elimination of All Forms of Discrimination Against Women. These documents have provided an important framework for combating violations against women and ethnic minorities, yet there has been little recognition in the international community that gay men and lesbians require – and deserve – similar protections. Although case studies demonstrate that a woman in prison may be singled out for rape because she is a lesbian, and although a man may suffer police violence because he is known to be homosexual or believed to carry the AIDS virus, human rights violations on the grounds of sexual identity are not yet expressly forbidden by any international law.

At the World Conference on Human Rights in Vienna, Amnesty International voiced its concern for the rights of sexual minorities in its proposals, specifying provisions for 'vulnerable groups which require greater attention within the human rights programmes including children, indigenous peoples, people with disabilities, religious, sexual, ethnic and linguistic minorities, and those afflicted by HIV and AIDS'. This proposal (not adopted as part of the final document created by the Vienna Conference) signals Amnesty International's belief that gay men and lesbians around the world remain at risk.

Fighting the battle for protection under existing laws

In theory, gay men and lesbians should enjoy the protection of the general human rights treaties, such as the International Covenant on Civil and Political Rights, and the International Covenant on Economic, Social and Cultural Rights which are intended to secure 'all rights for all people'. In some countries, sexual minorities have won legal protection for their rights on the basis of existing laws. The European Convention for the Protection of Human Rights and Fundamental Freedoms has already

provided a whole series of important decisions in favour of gay men and lesbian rights. In 1998, Senator David Norris, a longtime campaigner for homosexual rights, successfully argued that the Irish law which allowed the prosecution of consenting adults for homosexual acts was constitutionally invalid and in violation of the European Convention. The law in question was consequently struck from the books, as were similar laws in Northern Ireland following similar decisions.

At the same time, other countries are putting laws that specifically protect gays and lesbians into effect. In the United States, ten states now explicitly prohibit discrimination on the grounds of sexual orientation. And in May of 1996 the Republic of South Africa became the first nation to incorporate sexual orientation into the anti-discrimination provisions of its constitution.

Gays and lesbians remain at risk

Given the enhanced public awareness of gay and lesbian rights issues, given that some battles are being won in the courts, why is it that general human protections so often fail to shield gay men and lesbians from serious abuses?

First, many homosexuals who have been the victims of repression fail to report the violence against them. They may fear that their sexual

orientation may be made public as a result of speaking out, thereby laying them open to further violence and social ostracism. They may have a well-founded lack of trust in the authorities which should protect them, such as the police or social services. They may feel that their complaints will not be taken seriously or, worse, that their protest will bring down the wrath of those who harmed them, making them the target for serious reprisals. In many cultures, lesbians and gay men are so socially, culturally and economically marginalised that they lack the barest resources to defend themselves, call attention to their ill-treatment, or mobilise public opinion in their support. Lesbians may face double discrimination, because of their sex as well as their sexual orientation. The silence that grows out of such marginalisation and fear makes it difficult for concerned human rights agencies to monitor abuses or take action on the part of victims.

Next, discriminatory treatment of gays and lesbians is often 'masked', concealed behind bogus legal pretexts. In such cases, the victims may be officially charged with any number of offences in order to hide the true reasons behind their detention, imprisonment, torture of execution. 'Vagrancy', 'hooliganism', and 'unruly behaviour' are only a few examples of charges being used to bring sexual minorities under the power of the state. Once in custody,

they may be subject to extreme and unusual forms of abuse including false 'medical treatment' to 'cure' them of their 'illness'.

Because of age-old, deeply-held social and religious taboos, some governments are reluctant or unwilling to admit to the presence of gays and lesbians in their midst – let alone take steps to defend their human rights. They may see the issue of protections for gay rights as a foreign concept, forced on them by the domineering West. They may deny government involvement in abuse, turning a blind eye to violations and maintaining that, since private individuals are at fault, they can do nothing about them. Or, on the contrary, they may stridently defend their right to punish what they see as a criminal offence. Homosexuality, particularly sodomy between men, is still criminalised in many countries today. Same-sex relationships may be deemed 'deviant', 'unnatural', 'immoral', or 'against God's will'. Homosexuality is often believed to exert a corrupting, criminalising influence on minors, posing a threat to civic peace. It may be viewed as a 'foreign import' and as such subversive to traditional domestic values as well as social and political order. Homosexuals may be seen as a threat to 'family values' or to the fabric of society at large. The terror of AIDS and HIV infection has lent ammunition to many who hold such views – and has led to a new category of human rights violation: those targeting individuals because of their real or perceived HIV/AIDS status.

Governments who promote, fail to challenge, or attempt to disguise the persecution of gays and lesbians create a climate where abuses proliferate in secrecy beyond the reach of international human rights protections. In fairness, it should be said that human rights organisations and the international media have been slow to take up the cause of gay and lesbian rights. So, between the lack of specific international protections, the intractability of some governments, the failure of human rights organisations and the media to monitor violations, and their own reluctance or inability to report abuses, gay men and lesbians have too often found themselves the anonymous victims of oppression.

• The above is an extract from *Breaking the Silence*, produced by Amnesty International. See page 41 for address details.

Gays win sex at 16 battle

By Ewen MacAskill and Michael White

The Government signalled yesterday it will still contest in the European courts a move to legalise homosexuality in the armed forces, in spite of dropping a similar action over the age of consent.

Gay rights campaigners, who hold high hopes that Labour in government will prove more liberal than the Tories, celebrated the Government's dropping of opposition to a case in the European Court of Human Rights on the age of consent for homosexuals.

But campaigners had to temper their enthusiasm when it emerged that hopes of an early Commons vote on reducing the age of consent from 18 to 16 were receding.

Their enthusiasm was further diluted when the Ministry of Defence (MOD) indicated it will press ahead with a case in the European Court of Justice brought by a former naval officer who wants an end to discrimination in the armed forces.

Government will not contest age of consent case in Europe

Church edges toward more relaxed attitude on gay clergy

. . . but ban on homosexuals in the armed forces stays

The MoD opposes homosexuality in the armed forces, arguing it is bad for morale.

Peter Tatchell, spokesman for the gay rights group OutRage, said: 'It is very odd that the Government is now supporting gay equality on the age of consent in the European Court of Human Rights but opposing gay equality in the armed forces in the European Court of Justice.'

Welcoming the decision on the age of consent, he said: 'It is wrong that 16- and 17-year-old gay men are treated as criminals and threatened with up to two years' jail.'

In the last Commons vote in February 1994, MPs voted to reduce the age of consent from 21 to 18.

Although Conservative MPs yesterday condemned the prospect of it being reduced to 16, there is no obvious opportunity for a free vote in the next year or two.

The Government stressed its neutrality: it was only offering a free vote, not recommending reduction to 16. It had decided not to amend the law to lower the age of homosexual consent to 16 even though its out-of-court settlement in the European Court amounted to an admission that the law will not be enforced against 16- to 18-year-olds.

Whitehall officials confirmed there are no plans to allow MPs to vote to amend the Crime and Disorder Bill to reverse the 1994 Commons vote which lowered sexual rights for gays from 21 to only 18.

With all three main party leaders – including the Tories' William Hague – backing a lower age, ministers believe the change will come in time, but are in no rush to intervene, wary of the political minefield they would be entering.

While they are abandoning the Tory Government's defence in the case brought to the European Court with the backing of the gay rights group Stonewall, they are persisting in fighting cases brought for wrongful dismissal by gays forced out of the armed services.

The European Court case is regarded as 'bowing to the inevitable', but abandonment of the military cases might trigger the kind of row with the top brass which disfigured President Clinton's early months in office in 1992.

Officials say they are not implicitly warning the police not to prosecute 16- to 18-year-olds. But that is the conclusion chief constables seem likely to draw.

To further increase ministerial caution, senior ministers hold differing views, with Ann Taylor and David Blunkett voting for 18 in 1994. As with fox hunting, where the cabinet has no official policy that does not amount to a split. But Tony Blair will move carefully.

Tory MP for Maidstone, Ann Widdecombe, a former Home Office minister, insisted the Government ought to continue to defend the European Court case. 'I would have preferred the Government to have stuck to the law the British Parliament decided it wanted rather than to have caved in.'

'There was just a feeling that the law was making coming out even more difficult'
Chris Morris, gay campaigner

Chris Morris still won't say if he broke the law by taking a gay lover at 16, writes Maggie O'Kane. 'I weighed it up and I asked myself would I risk coming out and going to prison by saying I broke the law by having under-age sex. I decided no.'

No, but he did decide to embark on a risky two-year battle before the European Court of Human Rights. A battle for gay men in Britain to have the age of consent lowered to 16.

Mr Morris, now 18, is still at school in west London and plans to sit his A levels next year. Yesterday he talked about his delight at the news that the Government is to allow a free vote on lowering the age of consent. He went ahead with the action because he believed the Government had a case to answer in its treatment of gay men. 'I did it on the basis of equality. To say that to have sex at 16 was not criminal.

'I was 16. There was no big love story – just a feeling that the law was making coming out, which is really difficult for young gay men, even more difficult by making sex illegal.'

He went to the European Court with the support of his mother. He has no contact with his father. Mr Morris says he has also had the support of many of his school friends.

He insists there is no disappointment at losing the opportunity to fight the gay rights battle in the European Court. 'I'm much happier that it will be decided in Britain.'
© *The Guardian*
July, 1997

Discrimination in the workplace

Information from Stonewall

Evidence of discrimination
In 1993 Stonewall published a report, *Less Equal than Others*, based on a survey of 2,000 lesbians, gay men and bisexuals and their experience of discrimination at work. This report provided compelling evidence that discrimination, harassment and the closet are a problem for most lesbians and gay men at work:

Discrimination
16% of respondents (one in six) had faced discrimination at work because of their sexuality, and another one in five (21%) suspected they had been discriminated against because of their sexuality.

Harassment
48% of respondents (nearly half) had been harassed at work. Experiences included ostracism, being 'outed', false accusations of child abuse, blackmail, malicious jokes, threats and physical violence.

The closet
49% of respondents (nearly half) concealed their sexuality from some of the people they worked with. 19% (one in five) concealed their sexuality from everyone at work.

Independent evidence of discrimination
An independent report by Social and Community Planning Research (SCPR) confirms these findings. Their study, *Discrimination against Gay Men and Lesbians* (1995), was based on the first ever survey of a representative sample of lesbians, gay men and bisexuals. The study found:

Discrimination
4% had lost their job because of their sexuality and 8% had been refused promotion because of their sexuality.

Harassment
21% had been harassed at work

The closet
64% (two-thirds) concealed their

sexuality from some or all of the people they worked with.

SCPR also surveyed 600 heterosexuals, and found that one in three would be less likely to hire someone if they knew they were gay.

However, on the plus side, two out of three heterosexuals agreed that there should be a law against discrimination on the grounds of sexuality. This shows there is majority support for a new law against sexual orientation discrimination.

The lack of legal protection

Lesbians and gay men have virtually no protection from discrimination in law:

- Deciding not to appoint someone because of their sexuality is not unlawful.
- Treating someone less favourably because of their sexuality is not unlawful.
- Harassing someone because of their sexuality, or allowing other employees to harass them, is not unlawful.
- Paying someone less because of their sexuality is not unlawful (e.g. where an employer provides benefits for a spouse of heterosexual partners but refuses to recognise same-sex partners)
- Sacking someone because of their sexuality is not unlawful (unless a tribunal decides the dismissal is unfair – but you cannot claim for unfair dismissal unless you have worked for the employer for a minimum period of two years, and the leading case held it was OK to sack a gay man from a job involving even limited contact with children).

- Even a policy of sacking all known lesbians and gay men is not unlawful. The ban on lesbians and gay men in the armed forces was upheld as lawful by the Court of Appeal in 1995.

None of this discrimination would be lawful if the discrimination was based on sex, race or disability.

Stonewall and others have been arguing that sexual orientation discrimination is already unlawful because it amounts to a form of sex discrimination, because it involves an employer asking two questions: what sex are you?, and what sex is your partner?

However this argument was rejected by the European Court of Justice in the Lisa Grant case. Lisa Grant had argued that it was unlawful sex discrimination under the law on equal pay for her employers, South West Trains, to refuse a free travel pass to Lisa's partner Jill Percey because she was not an opposite-sex partner. The European Court said this was not sex discrimination but sexual orientation discrimination and was not covered by European Community law.

The Court noted that under a new provision of European community law, article 6A of the Treaty of Rome, the Community had the power to legislate to eliminate various forms of discrimination including discrimination based on sexual orientation, if it wished to. However article 6A provides that such legislation may be enacted only if all the member states agree to it unanimously. This is extremely unlikely to happen and so legislation by Parliament is now urgently needed.

The case for a law against discrimination

Unless Parliament passes a law against discrimination, the position now is that lesbians and gay men can be treated unfairly, harassed, paid less than others and even sacked, simply because they are gay.

The new law also needs to tackle discrimination against lesbians and gay men in areas other than employment, for example discrimination in education, and the provision of goods and services (in both public sector and private sector). The Sex Discrimination Act and the Race Relations Act make sex discrimination and race discrimination unlawful in all these areas. Lesbians and gay men need the same protection.

For example, the *Independent on Sunday* recently rang ten hotels featured in the *Which?* guide and tried to make a booking for a same-sex couple. Three of them refused. Hotels are not allowed to turn people away because they are black. Why should they be allowed to turn people away because they are gay?

Similarly, school and local authorities are under a duty not to discriminate on grounds of sex or race, and the Equal Opportunities Commission and the Commission for Racial Equality have powers to intervene if they do. Young lesbians and gays in the school system need the same protection.

The Sexual Orientation Discrimination Bill

This Bill would amend the Sex Discrimination Act to provide the same protection against sexual orientation discrimination as it already provides against sex discrimination. An earlier version of the Bill (dealing with employment discrimination only) was passed by the House of Lords on 1 May 1996 and was supported by the Labour front bench at the time. However it was never debated in the House of Commons.

Stonewall will now seek to have the Sexual Orientation Discrimination Bill re-tabled and we will be calling on the government to support this bill – as they did before the election

Labour's promises to end discrimination

Labour has repeatedly said it will tackle discrimination on grounds of sexual orientation:

'There should be no discrimination on the grounds of disability, gender, age, sexuality or race.' – Tony Blair, Leader of the Opposition, addressing Labour Party conference, October 1995.

'Labour believes that people should not be discharged from the military simply on the basis that they are gay . . . In government we will consult with the military on the practical issues involved in implementing change.' – Alun Michael, Home Affairs Minister covering lesbian and gay issues, responding to Stonewall's election campaign questionnaire.

Labour said in its election manifesto it was 'committed to ending unfair discrimination wherever it exists'.

And yet the Government sent lawyers to Luxembourg to argue against Lisa Grant's application. Although Lisa's case was against South West Trains, not the government, all member states have a right to make submissions in any proceedings before the Court and the government took advantage of this. Britain was the only country to send lawyers to argue against Lisa Grant before the European Court.

Lawyers for the British government argued that while they did not agree with discrimination on grounds of sexual orientation, this was a matter for legalisation, not litigation. The government now has a moral responsibility to put that legalisation before Parliament.

The government cannot pass the buck by looking to the European Community to legislate. Legislation at European level is extremely un-

likely since it would require the unanimous agreement of all 15 member states. The government has no control over the other 14 member states. It has full control over what happens in Parliament. It is time the government said whether it still believes that sexual orientation discrimination is unfair, and if so, what it is going to do about it and when.

What you can do . . .

. . . as a voter

Write to your MP and ask for his or her support for the Sexual Orientation Discrimination Bill. Explain what a difference such a law would mean to you personally.

If they are a backbencher, ask if they will table the Bill if they are placed in the Private Member's Bill Ballot.

Write to the Employment Secretary, Rt Hon David Blunkett MP, DfEE, Sanctuary Buildings, Great Smith Street, London SW1P 3BT, and ask if the government accepts that sexual orientation

discrimination is unfair, and if so when they will legislate to make it unlawful.

. . . if you are a trade union member

Ask your trade union to support the Sexual Orientation Discrimination Bill. Get a motion tabled at conference.

. . . if you are a Labour Party member

Raise the issue sexual orientation discrimination within the Party. When will the government keep its commitment to end this unfair discrimination?

. . . as a consumer

Write to the Association of Train Operating Companies, 24 Eversholt Street, London NW1, and ask them to extend the partner's travel concession on a national basis to same-sex partners on equal terms with heterosexual partners – in line with the equal opportunities policies of each of their members.

© Stonewall
March, 1998

Public opinion of lesbian and gay rights

SCPR's 1993 survey of 600 heterosexuals shows they thought that the following kinds of sexual relations were 'mostly' or 'always' wrong:

- in early teens – 78%
- extra-marital sex – 76%
- a single person with lots of partners – 55%
- two adult men – 51%
- two adult women – 49%
- a stable gay or lesbian couple – 35%
- sex before marriage – 11%

Equal rights

1991: 65% said that 'homosexual men and lesbians should have the same rights under the law as the rest of the population' (Harris).
1992: 71% agreed that 'gay men and lesbians should have the same rights under the law as everyone else' (Harris).
1995: 74% agreed that 'gay men and lesbians should have the same

rights under the law as everyone else' (Harris).

The criminal law

Percentage saying that homo-sexual relationships between consenting adults should be legal:
1977: 58% (SOC-Gallup)
1986: 48% (Harris)
1988: 48% (Harris)
1991: 66% said same sex acts should be legal (Gallup)
1992 74% said the age of consent should be the same for everyone, irrespective of their gender or sexual orientation. 86% agreed that 'Gay men found having sex in public should be subject to the same penalty under the law as heterosexual couples who are found in the same situation' (Harris).
1993 74% agreed that people should be allowed to have sex with any other consenting adult that they wish to, without interference from others (SCPR).

© Stonewall

Officials try to delay gays test case

By Lucy Ward, Political Correspondent

The Government is facing accusations of hypocrisy and delaying tactics after pressing European officials to postpone a test case challenging Britain's ban on homosexuals in the forces.

A confidential letter from a Foreign Office solicitor to the European Commission on Human Rights argues for a delay to a case brought by four former officers and due to be heard in the next few months.

The plea was yesterday dismissed by gay rights campaigners as a stalling tactic which could only 'perpetuate an existing injustice'. The four officers have already lost cases for unfair treatment in the High Court and Court of Appeal, brought in 1996.

The Government was anxious to stave off a potential compensation bill of up to £1 billion for homosexuals dismissed from the forces, critics claimed.

The letter from Foreign Office lawyer Martin Eaton calls for a delay to the former officers' case on the grounds that two of the four – ex-RAF nurse Jeanette Smith and former RAF administrator Graeme Grady – have launched industrial tribunal proceedings for unfair dismissal and sexual harassment.

Under European law an applicant must first exhaust all legal remedies in his or her home country.

A Foreign Office spokesman last night denied the Government was stalling.

However, Duncan Lustig-Prean, another of the four dismissed officers, called the intervention 'awe-inspiring hypocrisy by a government whose foreign policy hangs on human rights'.

Ministers made clear last October that they intended to fight to keep the ban on gays in the military. The Government is also contesting a case in the European Court of Justice by a former naval nurse, Terry Perkins, who argues that his dismissal was illegal under European employment law.

© The Guardian
January, 1998

Army's rethink over ban on gays

By David Fairhall, Defence Correspondent

The army is reconsidering its ban on homosexuality. A new code of personal conduct is being drafted which may make it possible for soldiers to admit to a homosexual orientation provided their conduct does not impinge directly on their unit's operational effectiveness.

The revised code, replacing a document published in 1993, has yet to be put to the Army Board. It would also need the approval of ministers.

But whereas the armed forces minister, Nicholas Soames, is opposed to any relaxation in the current ban on operational grounds, Labour is committed to reviewing the position if it wins the general election.

The Ministry of Defence is in any case under great pressure to change its policy, following changes in public attitudes that have led to legal challenges in the European courts.

'It's a question of whether we have a right to be different,' said one senior army source.

'Inevitably, a number of senior officers have discussed the position – not just homosexuality but sexual adventurism generally.

'They're looking at morality, at ethics and at ethos. But in the end this has to be a political decision.'

Defence sources emphasised that the internal paper on the revised code of conduct is still circulating at a relatively low level in the MoD and insisted that there was no question of anticipating a Labour general election victory.

Either way it makes good administrative as well as political sense for the army's top brass to sort out their own ideas and try to find agreement with the other two services before a new minister demands a review, or change is forced on them by a European Court ruling.

Many service chiefs believe some relaxation of the ban, perhaps along the lines of the 'don't ask, don't tell' compromise adopted by the American armed forces, is inevitable.

© The Guardian
March, 1997

Pay ruling gives gays equal rights in Europe

By Clare Dyer, Legal Correspondent

Homosexuals scored an 'historic' victory at the European Court of Justice in Luxembourg yesterday, in a test case over the denial of job perks to same-sex partners.

In a preliminary opinion, advocate general Michael Elmer held that South West Trains Ltd's denial of travel concessions to the woman partner of Lisa Grant, a ticket clerk, breached European law guaranteeing equal pay.

The case has far-reaching implications for employment rights in Britain. If the full court follows the opinion (which it does in four out of five cases), employers will have to offer same-sex partners the same perks, including pension benefits, available to unmarried partners of the opposite sex. Pay includes any benefits in cash or kind provided by an employer.

Ruth Harvey, Ms Grant's solicitor, said companies would have to look at all aspects of pay – salary, pensions, loans, mortgages and benefits – or risk claims against them.

However, the ruling could lead employers to limit perks to married partners. The advocate general held that this would not be contrary to EU law. Nor would it be unlawful under English law.

Ms Grant, aged 38, who lives in Southampton with her partner Jillian Percey, a nurse aged 30, went to an industrial tribunal after she was refused concessions worth £1,000 a year for Ms Percey. Her predecessor in the job had received free and cut-price travel for his unmarried female partner.

The case was referred by the tribunal to the European Court where Ms Grant, represented by Cherie Booth QC, claimed the refusal breached article 119 of the EC treaty which guarantees equal pay. After a definitive ruling by the court, the case will go back to the tribunal for a final decision in about six months.

The advocate general said yesterday that discrimination could not be justified on the basis that an employer wanted to benefit heterosexual but not homosexual couples. He also ruled that article 119 could be directly applied by courts and tribunals in Britain; if the full court agrees, this opens the way for tribunals to decide similar cases without reference to Europe.

Ms Percey said afterwards: 'We're ecstatic. It's more than we could have hoped for. Some companies give health insurance to partners and they [same-sex partners] will have that extended to them as well, as long as the opinion is upheld by the full court. We knew we were changing the law. It has been a hard campaign but well worth it.'

Angela Mason, director of Stonewall, which campaigns for equal rights for homosexuals, said: 'We are all absolutely delighted. This is an historic day for lesbian and gay rights, not just in this country but in the whole of the European Union.'

The opinion follows a ruling from the Luxembourg court extending protection from discrimination at work to transsexuals. Lawyers believe this paves the way for a similar ruling before long protecting homosexuals from any sort of discrimination at work.

Advocate general Elmer concluded: 'There is nothing in [EU law] to indicate that the rights and duties which result from the [law], including the right not to be discriminated against on the basis of gender, should not apply to homosexuals, to the handicapped, to persons of a particular ethnic origin, or to persons holding particular religious views.

'Equality before the law is a fundamental principle… The rights and duties which result from EU law apply to all without discrimination, and therefore also to the approximately 35 million citizens of the EU who are homosexual.'

© *The Guardian*
October, 1997

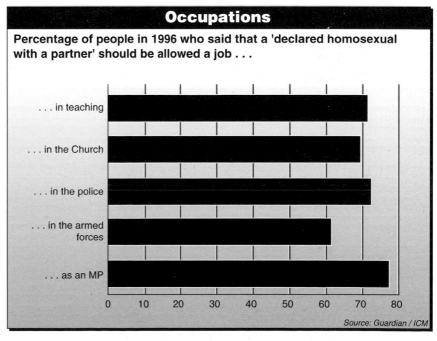

Occupations

Percentage of people in 1996 who said that a 'declared homosexual with a partner' should be allowed a job . . .

- . . . in teaching
- . . . in the Church
- . . . in the police
- . . . in the armed forces
- . . . as an MP

(scale: 0 10 20 30 40 50 60 70 80)

Source: Guardian / ICM

Gay civil servants win pension rights for their partners

Homosexual partners of civil servants are being offered pension rights. The move also extends the privilege, previously enjoyed only by a husband and wife, to thousands of heterosexual couples who are not married.

Instead of a marriage certificate, all a partner will need is proof of joint financial responsibility such as a bank account or a shared mortgage.

Gay activists greeted the Government's concession yesterday as 'a matter of fairness'.

But family campaigners protested that it amounted to a massive blow against the status of marriage. One said: 'The gay lobby is winning everything.'

Opponents fear it could set a precedent for three million other public sector workers, including the NHS, education and the police.

The pensions decision is also a signal to the gay lobby – which was offered a raft of new rights by New Labour during the General Election campaign – that Tony Blair and his colleagues are prepared to deliver.

Under long-standing rules, only widows or widowers of civil servants have been paid pensions after their spouse dies. They get payments that amount to about half the regular pension.

Chancellor of the Duchy of Lancaster David Clark, the Cabinet Minister in charge of the Civil Service, has ruled that the change to pension rules to allow unmarried partners the same rights as married people can go through.

But it is on the condition that civil servants are prepared to meet the cost themselves in the form of increased pension contributions.

Union leaders who are considering the offer are pressing the Government to meet the £20 million cost of the change itself.

By Steve Doughty, Social Affairs Correspondent

Valerie Riches of Family and Youth Concern said: 'This is another attack on marriage and the family, at a time when the Government should be doing everything it can to support the family.

'We know from a great deal of evidence that cohabiting relationships typically break up far more quickly than do marriages.'

She added: 'I do not understand how Mr Blair can go about with his Christianity emblazoned on his sleeve and yet appear to act against Christian principles in so much of what he does.

'The gay lobby is winning everything at the moment.'

The Stonewall pressure group welcomed the move. Spokesman Anya Palmer said: 'The Government promised fairness, and this is a matter of fairness.'

Labour has already said it plans to reduce the age of consent for homosexuals from 18 to 16, and Home Office civil servants are examining ways to allow gay partners the same immigration status as husbands or wives of Britons.

But some gay campaigners have protested at the slowness to act in other areas. For example, the Government has opposed the automatic granting to homosexual partners of rights given to spouses of employees.

The European Court is to give a preliminary ruling next week in a test case involving South West Trains worker Lisa Grant's attempt to win travel benefits for her lesbian partner.

Miss Grant's lawyer in the case is the Prime Minister's wife Cherie Blair, QC.

© *The Daily Mail*
September, 1997

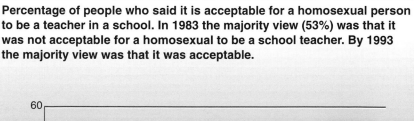

Lesbians and gay men at work

Percentage of people who said it is acceptable for a homosexual person to be a teacher in a school. In 1983 the majority view (53%) was that it was not acceptable for a homosexual to be a school teacher. By 1993 the majority view was that it was acceptable.

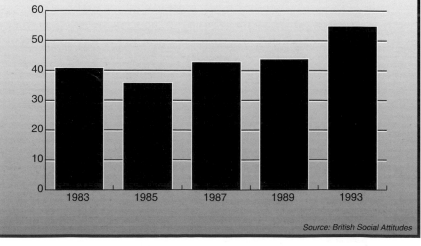

Source: British Social Attitudes

Playing it safe

A report detailing teachers' perceptions of the effects of Section 28 and their responses to bullying, sexuality and HIV and AIDS

The Terrence Higgins Trust, together with Stonewall, have commissioned a research project from the Health and Education Research Unit (HERU) – with a report, entitled *Playing it Safe*, published at the end of May 1997. The report examines issues related to homophobic bullying, teaching about sexuality and HIV and AIDS, as well as the perceived effects of Section 28 within schools.

The project involved distribution of a questionnaire to a random sample of a thousand schools in England and Wales. The response rate was 30.7% (n=307). In addition, telephone interviews were conducted with sixteen of the respondents, with some interesting, if not altogether unsurprising, findings.

82% of schools were aware of incidents of verbal homophobic bullying and 26% of physical bullying. Teachers themselves were also not immune to homophobic harassment. However schools accepted that homophobic comments were also perpetrated by teachers. One teacher believed that homophobia was more likely to be tolerated amongst staff than other forms of prejudice.

Some schools acknowledged that methods of monitoring bullying may affect their awareness of its prevalence, particularly as only 6% of schools had a bullying or discipline policy which included reference to lesbian and gay-related bullying. This falls to 5% for HIV and AIDS-related bullying in policies.

Lack of experienced staff was a primary factor affecting schools' ability to tackle homophobic bullying. But also parental disapproval, concern about the response of the local community and homophobia within staff teams were also cited as factors. Generally most schools were reluctant to identify homophobic bullying as requiring specific mention in policy documents. Lack of policy in relation to lesbian, gay and bisexual and HIV and AIDS related issues become clearer when examining other policies. For example, of the 289 respondents who provided information on equal opportunities policies, only a quarter made reference to sexuality (25%). This falls to 13% for HIV issues.

An area of particular policy confusion centred around Section 28. 75% were aware of this section of the Local Government Act but of these there was still a high degree of uncertainty about its implication. The majority (56%) stated that they had experienced difficulty in addressing the needs of lesbian, gay and bisexual pupils as a result of Section 28. Teachers were particularly confused about the notion of 'promoting homosexuality'. As a consequence, many had removed elements from the curriculum, including work tackling homophobic bullying.

Even where policies were in place and teaching about homosexuality undertaken, schools were keen to stress that it was not in any way promoted as a positive lifestyle. This is in spite of the fact that 61% of respondents were aware of lesbian, gay or bisexual pupils and 42% had been asked for help/advice about being lesbian, gay or bisexual. However, encouragingly 62% felt that schools were an appropriate setting for providing lesbian, gay or bisexual information.

The survey suggested that the large majority (95%) of schools addressed issues related to HIV and AIDS. However, findings concerning the needs of gay and bisexual pupils were complex and contradictory. One interviewee suggested that whilst HIV had made it more acceptable to discuss homosexuality, it also has the effect of limiting discussion to HIV and AIDS. In fact, often the only mention of homosexuality was during sex education – with lesbians and bisexuals largely being ignored completely. Many schools were of the opinion that addressing the specific needs of gay and bisexual pupils in relation to HIV would be inappropriate because gay and bisexual men and heterosexuals are at equal risk; while some teachers were concerned not to present AIDS as a 'disease of the gay community'. Both approaches could have the effect of denying the reality of the epidemic for gay and bisexual men.

The report further highlights the damage suffered by young gay and bisexual men, not only in terms of receiving inadequate information on HIV prevention, but also the long-term effects of bullying and the lack of support around sexuality. Depression, low self-esteem, guilt and shame are known to be linked to such school experiences, and are also known to be associated with people's ability to negotiate and maintain safer sex. Schools need to realise that they are failing some of their pupils, to such an extent, that significant numbers of young gay men are receiving an AIDS diagnosis during their early twenties. The report will hopefully alert schools to their damning failure and alert them to the need for change.

• The above is an extract from the *CHAPS Newsheet*, May/June 1997, produced by the Terrence Higgins Trust. See page 41 for address details.

© *Terrence Higgins Trust*
June, 1997

True colours

Choices for young men coming out

Am I gay or bisexual?

Do you have strong feelings for other men? Feelings of friendship or love? Sexual feelings? You might want to call yourself gay now. Or wait to see how you develop. If you have feelings for men and women you might want to call yourself bisexual. That's fine. It doesn't matter what you call yourself as long as you understand that being attracted to other men is perfectly OK.

You might be wondering why you have these feelings. It's nothing to do with how you were brought up. It's nothing to do with anything you've done – or didn't do. Or anything that anyone's done to you. It might be that people are just born gay or bisexual.

Lots of young people often have questions about their feelings towards their own sex.

But only you'll know with time if having these feelings for other men will always be a part of your life.

Having accepted that you are attracted to other men, you might want to know where to go from here. This information should help you.

You're not alone

If you realise you are gay or bisexual, then you're in good company. There are hundreds of thousands of men who are too. Black, white, Asian. Men of all races, religions and cultures, doing any job you can think of. You may know yourself of some famous actors, pop stars, sportsmen and politicians who are gay or bisexual – men who are happy, successful and proud of who they are.

So you're not on your own. If there's anything you feel the need to talk to someone about, ring a helpline mentioned at the end of this

information. You can talk to someone who'll understand.

Telling people

It's up to you who you tell about your feelings. You'll know best when to say anything and who to talk to. You don't have to tell anyone. But if you realise you're gay or bisexual and you tell people, it's often called 'coming out'.

Telling friends

- It can be a difficult thing to do but it often gets easier the more you do it. Afterwards it can be a big relief.
- Young people can be more understanding of gay and bisexual people.
- A lot of men find it easier to tell a female friend how they feel.
- Old friends can be easier to tell once you've already made new friends who understand you.
- You might lose some friends – they may be prejudiced or frightened of being labelled 'gay' themselves.

- But some friends might be proud that you chose to tell them.
- And true friends will stick by you whatever.

Telling your family

- Only you will know whether you want to tell your family about your feelings.
- It's a big step, but it can be well worth taking.
- Mums are often easier to tell than dads.
- The news might shock your family.
- Or they might have thought about it already.
- They may be fine about it.
- With time families often get used to the idea.
- You can tell people in a letter if that's easier.
- You might want to wait until you don't rely on your family for somewhere to live or to support you financially.
- A group called 'Parents' Friend' gives advice to families having difficulty accepting their gay and bisexual children. You could talk to them about telling your family.

School and afterwards

If you're still at school you'll have a good idea of what can happen if people find out someone's gay or bisexual. You'll know how safe it is to tell others at school.

- You could approach a sympathetic teacher if you find yourself being bullied or needing help.
- Many people decide to wait until they leave school when it gets easier to do what they want to.
- Your local lesbian and gay switchboard is there to offer you support.

After school you may go on to further education or start work. Moving away from home might make it easier to make a new start. Many colleges and universities have gay and bisexual social groups. These are a good way of meeting people.

If you're at work, only you'll know if coming out is right for you and who you might tell. Not everyone at work will be open-minded and accepting.

Meeting people

Here are ways to make contact with gay and bisexual people:
- Buying a gay magazine.
- Calling a lesbian and gay switchboard. They'll give you details of places and social groups in your area for gay and bisexual people.
- Gay and bisexual youth groups – just like regular youth groups, a good way of meeting people like yourself.
- Some people use gay chatlines – expensive to use and it'll show up on your phone bill that you've been phoning them (and be careful if arranging to meet strangers).
- Using the Internet.

Making contact with other people might not work out as you want first time round, but keep trying until you meet people you feel comfortable with.

Gay scene

Here are things about the gay scene to think about:
- There's a lot on offer – shops, pubs, clubs.
- These places are a lot like straight bars and clubs.
- Different places cater for different types of people.
- You can have a good time being with gay and bisexual people.
- Find out about a place before going – look in the gay press or phone a switchboard to find out what you need to know.
- You could check out an area in the daytime if you're not used to it.
- Going to a bar or club on your own probably isn't a good idea. It's a lot more fun going with a group.
- And safer. If you go home with

someone, you can let other people know where you're going.
- A good way to explore the gay scene is with people from one of the youth groups.

Drugs and drink

Drugs and alcohol can be a common part of the gay scene. Never be pushed into doing something that you don't want.

If you do drink alcohol or use drugs, make sure you know what their effects on you could be. They could affect your judgement, especially around having safer sex. Telephone helplines are a good source of information if you want to know more.

Life beyond the bars

There's more to life than pubs and clubs. There's a range of groups and things to do depending on where you live. Find out about them from the gay press or your local switchboard. There are groups for various interests – cultural, religious, hobbies and sports (e.g. swimming, football, rugby, badminton). There are gay community organisations you can get involved with too if you want.

The gay press

The gay press provides a link with other men like you. It has useful

information on current lesbian and gay issues and news about clubs, bars and events.
- You can find free gay newspapers, like *The Pink Paper*, in many public libraries, gay bookshops and gay bars.
- You can buy *Gay Times* in WH Smith and other newsagents.
- Some publications are also on the Internet. Here's one address: http://www.gaytimes.co.uk

Diversity

People in the gay communities come from many cultural backgrounds. If from an ethnic minority, you may find the same prejudices in the gay world as you do elsewhere.

Social groups and helplines exist for men from ethnic minorities, including those for black, Asian and Jewish people.

Although attitudes are changing, if you decide you're bisexual you may experience prejudice from some gay people. If you need to, you can talk to someone from a bisexual helpline and in some cities there are bisexual support groups.

Getting closer

Having sex should be fun and what you do sexually is your choice. Don't feel pressured into having sex or doing something you're not comfortable with.

Some people think gay sex must mean anal sex. You'll find lots of gay and bisexual men who don't want that. There are many other things to do, like masturbation and oral sex. Lots of people worry about being inexperienced – you're not the only one. We've all been there.

At the time of going to print (November 1997) the law is that you have to be 18 years old and over to have sex with another man.

HIV and AIDS

HIV is the virus that can lead to AIDS, and it can be passed on through sex. This is what you need to know to protect yourself:

- In men HIV can be in blood and semen.
- Sex that lets either of these two things into your body is a risk for HIV infection.
- Although HIV can affect anyone, a lot of gay and bisexual men have been infected with HIV.
- Having anal sex and not using a strong condom is the highest risk thing to do – for both partners.
- Oral sex may have caused a small number of men to become infected with HIV, but this seems rare.
- Oral sex is classed as 'safer sex'.
- To be extra safe avoid getting another man's semen in your mouth.
- There's no risk of HIV from kissing and masturbation.
- If you can, talk about safer sex to your partner before sex happens.

For more details about safer sex get a copy of The Terrence Higgins Trust leaflet *A guide to safer sex for gay and bisexual men*. Anything sent to you will be in an envelope that's discreet.

You can also ring The Terrence Higgins Trust Helpline or look at their web site at http://www.tht.org.uk and their site for gay and bisexual men at http://www.chaps.org.uk

Sexual health

If you're having sex it's a good idea to have regular check ups at a GUM (Genito-Urinary Medicine) clinic, also known as an STD (Sexually Transmitted Diseases) clinic. You can get checked for sexually transmitted infections and talk to someone about things like HIV. It may feel embarrassing at first but the staff are usually friendly and helpful. The service is free and confidential. Your parents or family doctor won't be told. If you think you have a sexually transmitted infection, it's best not to have sex with anyone until it's treated. You could ring your local gay switchboard for advice. They'll tell you where your local clinic is. Or you can ring the clinic straight away and make an appointment. Look in the phone book for the number, under 'Genito-Urinary Medicine' or 'Sexually Transmitted Diseases'.

Sexually transmitted infections

Safer sex should protect you from HIV, but it can't protect you from other infections like gonorrhoea, 'crabs', syphilis, scabies, genital warts, herpes, and hepatitis. 'Crabs' and scabies can be treated at home with lotions bought from chemists, but others will need to be treated at a clinic.

Hepatitis is a liver disease caused by a virus passed on through sex. It's a lot more infectious than HIV and lots of gay and bisexual men have become infected by it. Two types of hepatitis can be passed on through sex – A & B. Hepatitis B is more serious – sometimes it can be fatal. It can be passed on through kissing and oral sex, so it's a good idea to get vaccinated against it at a GUM clinic. There's no charge and it can save you from getting very ill. Ask about hepatitis A too. They'll tell you how it's spread and whether they can offer you the vaccination against it.

Condoms and lubricant

If you decide to have anal sex reduce the risk of HIV infection by using a condom.

- You'll need a strong condom like Durex Ultra Strong or Mates Super Strong (other condoms used for sex with women are too weak).
- You'll also need a lubricant and this must be water-based (like KY Jelly).
- Don't use oil-based things like baby oil, Vaseline, hand lotion, etc. as they weaken condoms.
- You can get condoms and lubricant in chemists.
- They're free in many gay bars and clubs.
- Carry some on you so you're always prepared.
- Practise with condoms on your own to get used to using them.

Relationships

Once you meet other gay and bisexual men you might have different sorts of relationships. You'll find having friends important. Perhaps you'll also have boyfriends. But being single is OK and not having sex is OK too. If you want to, you can choose to be part of a large gay and bisexual community as well.

If you find a boyfriend remember safer sex. Many men have become infected with HIV in relationships because they were in love and had unsafe sex without thinking about the risks.

Love is no protection against HIV – but safer sex is.

Living your life

If you decide you are gay or bisexual you can be sure of a lot of support. Hundreds of thousands of people are showing that you can be gay or bisexual and have a very happy, healthy and successful life. Your sexuality is just a part of who you are.

But it's a part of you that can bring lots of positive experiences and great people into your life!

Helplines

These numbers may be useful if you'd like to talk to someone in confidence. You might want to use a call box as helpline numbers can show up on your itemised phone bills.

Lesbian and gay switchboards

Look in your local phone book under the words 'lesbian and gay' or just 'gay'.

Most big towns and cities have gay switchboards. The number for London's switchboard is 0171 837 7324.

It's open 24 hours but it's very busy. Try one of the other switchboards if you can't get through.

© The Terrence Higgins Trust 1998

The social implications

Information from The Maranatha Community, a movement of Christians in all the main churches

Society's perceptions

For centuries Western society generally regarded the homosexual act as unnatural, unacceptable and anti-social. Although there was widespread disapproval of the homosexual act, politicians, prompted by and with the active support of vociferous pressure groups, introduced the 1967 Sexual Offences Act which decriminalised the homosexual act for consenting adults over the age of 21. The primary argument for this was the claimed need for the individual to be protected from blackmail and from unwarranted intrusion into his or her private life.

Society's reaction

Since the decriminalisation of homosexual acts in this and in other countries there has been a sustained political campaign by homosexual organisations to present homosexual behaviour as normal and homosexuality itself as inborn and irreversible. 'Gay' groups have actively encouraged practising homosexuals to 'come out' and publicly announce their sexual preferences. In spite of this there remains considerable public concern about the homosexual act.

- 70% of men believe that homosexual practice is always or mostly wrong according to one of the most detailed studies yet carried out – (*British Sexual Attitudes*, Wellings K et al. Penguin, 1994, pages 183, 253).

The nature of homosexuality

Homosexuality, being a condition of people who have a sexual attraction to those of the same gender, may, or may not be a temporary or life-long preference or practice. It may or may not result in a sex act. There is no reliable evidence of it being a genetic inheritance and there is considerable

evidence of people moving into normal sexuality after receiving appropriate help or therapy. Most young people during the process of maturing go through periods of same-sex affection which gay activists wrongly classify as a permanent state of homosexuality.

- 'Few people pass through life without at some stage experiencing homosexual feelings' (J J West – *Homosexuality Re-examined*).
- 'The mis-information spread by certain circles that "homosexuality is untreatable by psychotherapy" does incalculable harm to thousands of men and women' (Dr R Fine, *Psychoanalytic Theory, Male & Female Homosexuality: Psychological Approaches* 1987).

Homosexuality and the family unit

The family is the basic unit of society. Relationships between homosexuals are founded on personal sexual preference, whereas the traditional heterosexual marriage is not merely a private arrangement between two people, but a social contract and a security for our children. The basic purpose of marriage is to provide children with a stable, secure and balanced family in which they can discover their identity and grow to maturity.

It is beyond dispute that children need the male and female role models which their fathers and mothers provide. Children need a safe, long-term environment in which to develop and grow into mature adulthood and true gender identity. Current moves to introduce legally recognised homosexual 'marriages' and to allow the adoption or fostering of children by cohabiting homosexual couples, raise grave issues of public morality and the care of children – particularly those who may already be damaged.

Those who resist gay demands are often subjected to vilification, and labelled as 'homophobic' or bigoted.

- The Chairman of Hackney Social Services threatened that any parent who does not want their child to be fostered by a homosexual would be 'counselled' by his staff. (8.1.85)

For the sake of 'gay rights', children are in danger of being deprived of the right to have healthy male and female role models, and to be protected from potentially confusing and even damaging influences. Single-sex partnerships of whatever nature fail to provide this.

There is in fact a profound antagonism to the concept of traditional marriage and family amongst some militant homosexual organisations.

- 'We must aim at the abolition of the family' (declaration in the *Gay Liberation Front manifesto 1971 & 1976*).
- The best scientific evidence suggests that putting society's stamp of approval on homosexual partnerships would harm society in general and homosexuals in particular, the very individuals some contend would be helped. (*Same Sex Marriage, 'Til Death us do Part?'* Family Research Institute Inc. Colorado Springs).

The quality of homosexual relationships

Broken, damaged, superficial or non-existent human relationships lie at the root of many of society's problems today. A high proportion of all homosexual relationships are temporary, many transient. Long-term, 'stable', and single-partner homosexual partnerships, although they do exist, are comparatively rare.

To a seemingly greater extent than in heterosexual relationships, many homosexual friendships are particularly fraught with jealousies, angers, tensions, and hypersensitivity to criticism and competition. This may be generated or exacerbated by widespread multi-partnering which is such a pronounced feature of homosexual culture.

One of the fundamental characteristics of the emerging 'gay culture' is the open promotion and encouragement of promiscuity and what appears to be a gross obsession with the sex act. This is evidenced in numerous gay publications.

Homosexual partnerships have a high rate of domestic violence, seriously affect health and longevity. Some active homosexuals are deeply unhappy in their condition and way of life and would wish to change if it were possible.

The promotion of homosexuality

The issue of homosexuality is being given increasing prominence today in this and other countries by virtue of militant political campaigning by homosexual organisations. These groups now exercise a disproportionate influence in the media, local government, Parliament and social services. They receive very substantial public funding, both nationally and internationally. Events promoting and 'celebrating' the gay lifestyle have received huge sums of money from local councils, statutory bodies, commercial organisations and the national lottery.

- One Council, GLC, gave over one million pounds to gay groups between 1981 and May 1984 (Rachel Tingle, *Gay Lessons*, Pickwick Books).

The major campaigns of homosexual organisations are directed at achieving legislative changes which would strengthen the position of homosexuals in society, and are also aimed at establishing total public acceptability of homosexual behaviour on the basis of it being deemed normal rather than deviant.

- The above is an extract from *Homosexuality – The Medical, Social and Religious Implications*, produced by The Maranatha Community.

When a son breaks the news he is gay

Reports by Michael Streeter

The mother's story

Shocked: he was so popular with girls
Anne Marie Blakey was shocked when her 16-year-old son Peter walked into the shop where she was working and 'blurted out' that he was gay.

'I had never suspected he might be, he was always very popular with the girls,' said Mrs Blakey, who works in a fruit and vegetable store in Consett, Co Durham. 'He just shouted it out in front of everyone. I told him I couldn't get my head around it at work, that I'd talk to him that evening. I think he thought I was going to be angry with him.'

After a night of tears and talking, the family began to come to terms with their only child's announcement. Mrs Blakey, 39, now looks at the arguments for lowering the age of consent for gay sex in relation to Peter's experiences, and unreservedly backs the call for equality.

'It was only later that I realised what Peter had been through at school, on his own,' she said. 'He told me other boys had a go at him, but I never knew.

'I think he has handled it very well and it shows he was mature enough. I'm very proud of him.'

She added: 'I can't believe it's right that a 16-year-old is not old enough to have a relationship with another man but is old enough to get a girl pregnant and run off and leave the child.'

She said she had never suspected that Peter was gay until his announcement, and that he seemed to have many girlfriends when he was younger. 'Obviously, looking back they were not that kind of girlfriend.'

Many other young people who come out are less fortunate in the reaction of their parents, and Mrs Blakey has a message for such families. 'Please do not throw your children out – keep the family together. Let them express their feelings, but remember they are still your children.'

Elsewhere in the north-east, Pat Atthey knows just how badly parents can react to the news their children are gay.

She set up a support group for parents of gay and lesbian children after being ashamed at her own reaction to the discovery her youngest son, Rob, was gay. 'I just had stereotypes in my mind, like the John Inman character in [the television comedy] *Are You Being Served?* I thought that my normal young son – the youngest and my baby – was going to change in some way.

'I didn't realise that Rob did not choose to be gay – it chose him.'

Mrs Atthey said some parents felt 'disgusted and alienated' when offspring broke the news, though most of these were reconciled within a few months. 'Parents, especially mothers, tend to want to blame something or someone. Often a mother will say, what have I done wrong, or differently from before? But everything falls into place if you accept that people don't choose it.'

The son's story

A cry for help: but they took it well
Care worker Peter Blakey, now just 18, recalls with relief how his mother and father accepted the revelation that he was gay.

Speaking from his family home in Consett, Co Durham, Peter described the anguish he went through before revealing his true sexual orientation not long after his sixteenth birthday.

'It took me about a month to pluck up the courage to tell them.

'I told people at college straightaway when I went there in the September, but it was October before I told my mother. I never

wanted to tell my dad because I thought it would finish everything, that it would end things between us.

'I went to see my mum at work during my lunch break and I just blurted it out. It was just like a cry for help on my part.

'Parents, especially mothers, tend to want to blame something or someone. Often a mother will say, what have I done wrong, or differently from before?'

'I had no idea they would take it so well.

'I knew that for them it would mean no grandchildren, no weddings, no daughter-in-law and all that.

'Well, I suppose I thought mum would be all right about it, but not as good as she's been. Since then they've both been great.'

Peter was pleasantly surprised how his straight friends at college – mostly female – had accepted his news.

'They seemed fine about it, they reacted as if they had always known. They talk about it quite openly.'

However, one male friend in their group reacted differently. 'We never told him about it directly, he

just knew about it. He moved away from us.'

Peter now supports the current move towards lowering the age of consent, even though he says some older men are particularly attracted to younger boys. 'I think I can understand some of the concerns. I have been to places in Newcastle and Manchester and some of the older guys prefer the younger ones.

'But I'd known I was gay since about 13 or 14. The hardest thing, in fact, is coming out and telling people, not knowing your own mind,' he said.

'Some guys around 16 or 17 are starting to experience what's going on, to see what it's like. I don't see any problem with that.'

He takes a philosophical approach towards his sexuality. 'As far as I'm concerned it's no big deal. It's just the way I am, and it is simply a question of coming to terms with it.'

Despite Peter's most positive experiences, a significant proportion of gay and lesbian youths – one in 10 according to a 1980s survey – are forced to leave home because of their parents' reaction. Peter Tatchell, of the campaign group Out-Rage!, says a new phenomenon is that many gays and lesbians are coming out younger than ever, between 13 to 15 when sex would still be illegal under the likely changes in the law.

'No one's really picked up on this so far. These groups are still in danger of being criminalised,' he said.

© *The Independent*
July, 1997

Gay rights have gone far enough

By Leo McKinstry

This weekend, an estimated 250,000 people gathered in London for the annual Gay Pride festival. This year, the event had extra cause for celebration, for it is the 30th anniversary of the 1967 Sexual Offences Act, which legalised homosexuality.

In the intervening three decades, we have, thankfully, become an increasingly tolerant society. Where once it was a crime, homosexuality is no longer even a barrier to advancement in public life. In Chris Smith, we have Britain's first openly gay Cabinet Minister, while the 1997 General Election saw the election of two other openly gay MPs.

Bigotry against gays is fast disappearing in other ways. In the media and arts, stars like Sir Ian McKellen feel no need to be secretive about their gay orientation. Businesses now target gay consumers, who are often wealthier than heterosexuals because of the absence of family commitments. We have advertising aimed at gays, gay sections in bookshops, even gay-dominated shopping precincts like Soho in London.

Such developments are to be welcomed. No one should be discriminated against because of their sexuality. And as a former Islington councillor, who used to chair the Equal Opportunities Committee and campaigned in the past for Chris Smith, I have little time for anti-gay prejudice.

But there is a great difference between opposing discrimination and supporting the whole agenda of gay rights that campaigners now demand.

This agenda, including calls for gay marriages, gay sex education in schools, and a lower age of consent, is based on the concept that every form of sexual behaviour is valid and should be respected, no matter how promiscuous or bizarre. This outlook is the dominant creed of our age, but it has damaging consequences for our society.

Take marriage and the family. In the brave new world of gay rights, no moral distinction is made between the sacrifices involved in bringing up children within a stable relationship and irresponsible hedonism. Both are presented as just different lifestyle choices. Such a disastrous message is now being given out to schoolchildren.

> **There is a great difference between opposing discrimination and supporting the whole agenda of gay rights that campaigners now demand**

Last year, for example, Camden and Islington Health Authority produced, at a cost of £40,000, a booklet entitled *Colours Of The Rainbow* for children aged five to 16,

which encouraged them 'to be positive about being gay'. The author boasted: 'Homosexuality and bisexuality have been put on the agenda as acceptable ways of life.'

Our gay rights egalitarians and sex educators appear to have lost all notions of both morality and childhood innocence. But what is even worse is the way that the modernist demand for 'sexual emancipation' has left children vulnerable.

For in the warped climate of explicitness, where all moral boundaries have dissolved, it is not difficult for paedophiles to develop an internal justification for their actions. After all, what are they doing but expressing their own sexuality? On June 26, Peter Tatchell, the grotesque gay rights extremist, could be found in *The Guardian* defending the publication by the Gay Men's Press of a book called *Dares To Speak*, which, unbelievably, argues for more freedom for paedophiles. Tatchell has also consistently campaigned for the age of consent to be reduced to 14, claiming: 'The sexual health of young people is best ensured by empowerment rather than repression.'

This ideology has badly undermined our child protection services, allowing abusers to exploit the system. In the notorious Islington child abuse scandal, the independent inquiry found management was reluctant to act on allegations of abuse for fear of appearing 'homophobic' or 'judgmental'.

It is ironic the desire to counter 'sexual prejudice' should have resulted in the brutal oppression of innocent children.

The gay rights campaigners might demand equality in public services, but so often what they end up with is special treatment. This is because we live in the age of the victim, where certain 'disadvantaged groups' are deemed worthy of extra support from the public purse.

Last week, Warrington Health-care Trust advertised for a Lesbian and Gay Youth Development Worker whose job aims to: 'Empower young lesbians and gay men as a group to address their expressed needs.' Among this year's grants from the Arts Council was £118,000 to the Gay Sweatshop Theatre Company, while the North West Arts Board gave almost £25,000 to the event It's Queer Up North.

Some of the worst of this sort of activity takes place under the guise of health promotion. In the name of 'raising awareness around issues of sexual health', the taxpayer has ended up subsidising the most extreme of gay lifestyles.

Lambeth, Southwark and Lewisham Health Authority gives £43,700 to an outfit called BIG UP ('Black Men Delivering HIV/Aids Information to Black Gay and Bisexual Men').

Among the group's recent events have been Give Him Something He Can Feel, 'a safer sex

---

The gay rights campaigners might demand equality in public services, but so often what they end up with is special treatment

---

extravaganza' and Come Play With Me, 'an afternoon of toys, games and fantasy for black gay and bisexual men'.

There are also notorious 'cottaging and cruising projects' dotted round the country, where public servants hand out condoms in gents' toilets and parks to gay men seeking a good time with total strangers. The campaign group, Gay Men Fighting Aids, which receives public funding of over £250,00, holds workshops on 'Bondage for Beginners', runs 'Sado-Masochism Sex Days', and provides 'tips on running a successful orgy'.

All this is hardly evidence of a society bent on discrimination against gays. Instead, our policy-makers have become so terrified of accusations of prejudice they are unwilling to defend any values of restraint against the tide of self-gratification.

And this brings us to one of the central problems with the gay culture. Because the only thing gays and lesbians have in common is their sexuality, the gay world is obsessed with sex. But this has created a terrible narrowness of focus.

As Paul Burston, who edits the gay pages of *Time Out*, the London listings magazine, has said: 'Basing your whole identity on what you do in bed, and how often, is rather sad.'

Instead of wallowing in the cosy hedonism of their victim-fixated existences, the gay rights extremists should face up to the real responsibilities of life in modern Britain. Then they would achieve something in which they could really take pride.

© Leo McKinstry
The Daily Mail, July, 1997

Gay couples 'too few to be counted'

By Steve Doughty, Social Affairs Correspondent

An official survey to discover how many homosexuals live together as couples was shelved – because it found so few.

Analysts dropped the project when out of 9,700 households, they found only 14 avowedly gay male or female couples.

Homosexual pressure groups frequently cite claims that one in ten of the population is gay and are pressing heavily for homosexuals to be given the right to marry.

But according to figures collected for the Government's General Household Survey, which is intended to give a definitive picture of how Britons live, only 0.0014 per cent of the population lives in a homosexual household.

The figures, revealed yesterday, were collected two years ago, when interviewers spoke to more than 18,000 people in 9,700 homes.

Statisticians planned to include figures on gay households when the full results were published earlier this year but the idea was dropped, they said, because the researchers found so few. John Haskey, of the Office for National Statistics, which conducts the survey, said: 'We were surprised by the small number of homosexual couples.

'It is possible people didn't want to reveal the information. But we know that in the past some such couples have definitely wanted to record the information.'

The 'gay' question, directed at

people of the same sex, was: 'Are you living together as a couple?'

If the answer was Yes, interviewers noted the couple as 'same sex co-habitants'.

Mr Haskey said: 'It was a pretty neutral question. People know what it means. They don't misinterpret it.'

In a survey calibrated to take in all regions and all social groups, the researchers found one gay couple for every 692 homes they visited – one-seventh of one per cent of all homes.

If the same applies to the country as a whole, fewer than 100,000 out of a population of 58.4 million are living in stable homosexual relationships.

© *The Daily Mail*
September, 1997

'The best option is to be open'

Environment minister Angela Eagle tells Suzanne Moore why she decided to reveal that she is a lesbian

Everyone you talk to says Angela Eagle will go far. She is seen as highly talented and exceptionally hard-working by all her colleagues. She is also spoken of as a somewhat serious and private person.

Few know that she is a passionate music and sports fan, happier in jeans backstage at an Elvis Costello concert than in the suits she first started wearing to make herself 'look older'. We begin, inevitably, talking about the extraordinary events of the past two weeks.

She is the same age as Diana, Princess of Wales was – 36 – and cried her eyes out watching the funeral. 'There is something very important about what Diana has come to represent. The female side of things has come to the fore,' she says.

Angela is well placed to see how the culture of Westminster reflects this, and how it has changed with the intake of new women MPs, as she has been there since 1992. 'When I first came here, it was like walking into one of those clubs in Pall Mall. I was forever going into rooms marked Members Only and finding that they were urinals, and was always being mistaken for a secretary. Bur a lot of these assumptions had already started to change.

'Having a female Speaker has made a huge difference. The changes have been gradual, but now it feels as though there is a rush on. Having a female Leader of the House is tremendously important and Ann Taylor is well keyed into how Parliament, as an institution, needs to change its workings. That means everything – from the hours to how the day is organised.

'Like all the royal protocol that has caused so much trouble this week, we have our own ridiculous protocol. For instance, there is a rule that you have to wear a top hat to make a point of order during a vote. Traditionalists love it, but it's stupid; it makes us look stupid and nobody understands it.'

She describes the moment when Tony Blair first came into the house as Prime Minister. 'Everyone clapped, but you are not allowed to clap. The new MPs didn't know that and they just did it. So that was that one out of the way.

'At Question Time now, I can see the women looking slightly embarrassed. That's a huge change from the shouting and leering that there used to be.'

Interestingly, Angela doesn't go along with the view that Parliament needs to be more women friendly; rather, she uses the expression 'people friendly'.

'I care about politics deeply. To change the world, or at least a little part of it, you have to come in here to do your job. It's not that I'm whinging – I love this job – but you have to give up so much of your life to get into that position. Even as a backbencher, you can easily work 24 hours a day. Yet everybody needs to have another life, so that they can be more balanced and have some insight into the people they are representing.'

She is very wary of becoming 'institutionalised'. 'With your life as an MP, it is very difficult to maintain relationships. Look at the high divorce rates here. There is a lot of pressure on your family. Just because you have signed up for this job, there is an assumption that your whole family has as well. When I was first elected, I got some very moving letters from the children of former MPs saying: "If you have a family, please do not do to them what [my mother/father] did to me." We need to be more tolerant of MPs trying to maintain their family and personal lives.'

So how does she manage hers? 'I have a long-term and very happy relationship, but sometimes I don't know how we find the time to see each other. You have to think not only about your partner, but their family and your own.

'In my case, I happen to be with a woman and I think I've only been able to cope with that because I have a very understanding family. My sister [Maria Eagle is Angela's twin and

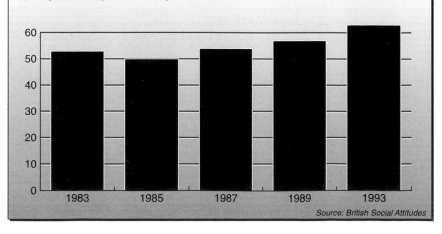

Responsible positions

Percentage who said it is acceptable for a homosexual person to hold a responsible position in public life:

Source: British Social Attitudes

also an MP], my brother and my father, all of whom are hetero-sexual, have always supported me. And that definitely has made that aspect of my life much easier to cope with.'

Until now, Angela has not ventured this information about her sexuality to her constituents, but says she would have told anyone who asked. 'I think people should look at you for the values you represent and the way you do your job locally. I don't think my sexuality has a direct relevance on those things.'

Several members of the party know that she is gay and have also been very supportive. 'To be honest, I didn't expect anything different. Attitudes have changed. The funny thing is that all the straight men I've told haven't been the least bit surprised. Most of the gay men were gobsmacked. I suspect that the straight men realise that you are not flirting with them; gay men, bless them, don't notice.'

Her decision to come out, she says, depended on two things; first, dealing with it herself, and, second, feeling the need 'to get a handle on this job and make sure that I can do it properly. I am at the stage where I need to get things sorted so I can just concentrate on my work.'

As the only open lesbian in the House, and a minister to boot, she certainly doesn't want to be seen as simply a spokesperson for gay rights. 'That's just one aspect of what I'm about. I've always supported gay rights to the extent that I believe gay people should have the same civil rights, equal rights, partnership rights and the right to be free from irrational discrimination as everyone else. I've always voted that way whenever such issues arose. Then again, my sister feels the same way and she isn't gay.'

She is more than aware that many gay people have not received the kind of personal or political support she has. 'It's obviously harder for gay people to be open. Some cannot be "out" at work; it's not illegal to sack people for being gay. And it must be really hard to cope when your parents, the people who are meant to help you through life, have a major problem with you. I realise how lucky I have been.'

Other MPs, I am sure, will be watching the public reaction to her openness before they make their own decisions to be as honest

---

So will we be seeing Angela and her partner at official occasions, the way we see Chris Smith and his?

She smiles. 'My partner has never expressed any wish to come. She is actually very busy with her own life, and I've always done pretty well without her there.'

I wonder how much of a strain this has been on her. 'Obviously, when I was first elected it was, personally, quite difficult. I mean, we know people, long-standing Members of Parliament, who have never been truthful, but I think times have changed and the best option now is to be open about it.'

Has she been at all concerned that her sexuality would, in any way, be a bar to promotion within the party?

'I get no sense of that at all. I think people are more sensible than we sometimes give them credit for.' Other MPs, I am sure, will be watching the public reaction to her openness before they make their own decisions to be as honest.

'I think the most significant thing is for an MP to operate as a well-rounded person. Relationships are the most important things in our lives; so is doing a good job and so is our happiness.

'There has been this prurient, almost puritanical attitude to politicians in the past. But the question now is: should politicians be human beings? And I say yes, we should be. I'd rather be governed by human beings than perfect cardboard cut-outs.'

Is it safe to come out now?

Owning up to homosexuality used to be political suicide. Alice Thomson reports.

With 416 Labour MPs in the new Parliament, standing out from the crowd can be difficult. But Angela Eagle will have no such problem. Not only is she the first MP to have a twin sister in the House, but she is now Britain's first self-confessed lesbian minister. 'Attitudes have changed,' she says. 'The time is right to be open.'

For years, rumours about closet homosexuals in the Palace of Westminster have been rife. But politicians were as likely to announce their homosexuality as to be caught spitting at a baby. Six months ago, Ian Greer, himself homosexual, suggested that there were as many as 40 homosexual MPs. Only five have gone public and all except one are Labour.

Before the 1967 Sexual Offences Act – legalising homosexuality between consenting adults – any such confession was political suicide. Ian Harvey, a talented Tory MP in the Fifties, ruined his career when he was caught with a guardsman in St James's Park. Tom Driberg, pillar of the Labour Left, was a promiscuous homosexual but he never ack-nowledged it publicly.

Even in the Eighties, MPs admitting to homosexuality usually resigned the next day. Matthew Parris, sketch writer for *The Times*, triggered a by-election in his West Derbyshire seat, and Harvey Proctor retired to run a shirt shop when he was outed.

The mood began to change under John Major. After disclosures in the *News of the World*, Michael Brown, Tory MP for Brigg and Cleethorpes, resigned as a Govern-ment whip – but remained an MP.

Tony Blair has been determined to go one step further. Chris Smith has been made the first openly male homosexual Cabinet minister; two new Labour MPs, Ben Bradshaw and Stephen Twigg, have been told that their admission of their sexual preferences will be no bar to promotion.

But many traditional MPs on both sides are still squeamish about the subject. 'If an MP says he or she is gay and they are in a long-term relationship, most people accept it,' says one former Tory minister. 'But some homosexuals are promiscuous, and they can be a political problem.'

The medical implications

Everyone has an equal right to health care and also the right to be informed of facts which could affect their choices in adopting a healthy lifestyle. These notes express serious health concerns about the homosexual lifestyle

Definition

A homosexual is a person who has a sexual attraction to a person of the same sex. A distinction must be drawn between individuals who experience homosexual attraction and those who also enter into sexual relationships with partners of the same sex. There is clearly a difference in the health risks likely to be encountered within a stable, life-long monogamous relationship and those who engaged in temporary relationships with multiple partners.

Prevalence

Studies carried out in USA and UK suggest a consistent figure of less than 1.5% of the adult population to be actively homosexual.

- One of the most detailed UK studies showed only 0.4% of the male population to be exclusively homosexual (Welling K., Field J. et al, *Sexual Behaviour in Britain*; Penguin 1994:183, 253).
- A survey in the United Kingdom sponsored by the Wellcome Trust reported 1.4% of males having had a homosexual partner in the previous year. The report stated its findings 'were consistent with those from other recent studies in Europe and the United States'. A British survey in 1990-1991 (among 19,000 men) found that 1.1% had had homosexual partners in the previous year (Johnson A.M. et al, Sexual Lifestyles & HIV risk; *Nature*; 360, Dec. 3rd 1992).
- An official survey of sexual behaviour showed that 98.5% of adults were exclusively heterosexual. Less than 1% had been exclusively homosexual since the age of 18 years. (UK Government General Social Survey by Prof. Tom Smith, University of Chicago 1989)

Causative factors

The origin of the homosexual condition is not fully understood but there is considerable evidence to point to it being an acquired or learned behaviour rooted in confusion of identity and/or childhood or adolescent trauma. There is no reliable evidence to suggest that it is due to organic or genetic factors.

- In March 1993 two psychiatrists of Columbia University reviewed studies purporting to find a biological component to homosexuality. They concluded 'there is no evidence at present to substantiate a biologic theory' (Byne and Parsons, Human sexual orientation: The Biological Theories reappraised; *Archives of General Psychology*; Mar 93, 50:228-239).
- Lawrence Hatterer, American psychiatrist, states 'homosexuals are not born but made and genetic, hereditary, constitutional, glandular or hormonal factors have no significance in causing homosexuality'. Dr Frank Lake, psychiatrist, discovered considerable evidence of the significance of disorders in infant years being directly related to the homosexual condition. Dr Charles W. Socarides, Clinical Professor of Psychiatry at the

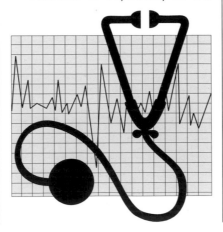

Albert Einstein College of Medicine in New York, has stated that homosexuality is not innate, but is learned behaviour.

- Dr John Money of the John Hopkins School of Medicine and Director of the Psychohormonal Research Unit states 'whatever may be in the possible unlearned assistance from constitutional sources, the child's psychosexual identity is not written, unlearned in the genetic code, the hormonal system or the nervous system at birth.'
- Dr Elizabeth Moberly, psychologist and authority on homosexuality, regards homosexuality as 'essentially a state of incomplete development or of unmet needs'. She asserts that homosexual orientation is rooted in 'same-sex psychological deficits' and arises from 'difficulties in the parent-child relationship, especially in the earlier years of life'.

Lifestyle characteristics

Homosexual relationships are usually temporary. Long-term, 'stable', and single-partner homosexual partnerships are exceptional. One of the characteristics of the emergence of the 'gay culture' has been the open promotion and encouragement of the high level of promiscuity which is a feature of male homosexuality. Some studies cite men having up to 25 sexual partners per day.

- 74% of male homosexuals reported having more than 100 partners during their lifetime; 65% reported having sex only once with more than half their partners; 28% reported having more than 1000 partners. 10% of homosexuals and 28% of lesbians claim to be close-coupled (quasi marriage): (Bell & Weinberg, *Homosexualities; A Study of Diversity among Men and Women*, New York: Simon & Schuster, 1978: 308, 346).

- 7% have a relationship lasting longer than 10 years.
  38% have never been in a relationship lasting longer than 1 year (Saghir & Robins, *Male & Female Homosexuality: A Comprehensive Investigation* – Baltimore: William Wilkins, 1973).

- 14% of homosexual men in San Francisco reported a single sexual partner in the previous year (1992). The vast majority had multiple sex partners (Osmond, D. H. et al, *American Journal of Public Health*; 1994, 84: 1933-37).

- In Denmark, a form of homosexual marriage has been legalised since 1989. By 1995, less than 5% of Danish homosexuals had married and 28% of these marriages had already ended in divorce or death (Wockner; *Advocate*; 726 Feb. 4 1997: 26).

- 69% of Dutch gays with a marriage-type 'partner' actually lived together. The average number of 'outside partners' per year of 'marriage' was 7.1 and increased from 2.5 in the first year of the relationship to 11 in the sixth year (Deenan et al, *Archives Sexual Behaviour*; 1994, 23: 421-431)

- Perhaps half of lesbians live together in monogamous relationships. These typically dissolve in one to three years (*Same Sex Marriage, Til Death Us Do Part?*, Family Research Institute).

It is widely recognised that homosexual relationships are frequently characterised by tension, jealousy and hypersensitivity, inevitably exacerbated by multipartnering. Surveys have shown that homosexual partnerships have the highest rate of domestic violence.

- In the 1992 SIGMA study funded by the Medical Research Council and the Department of Health no fewer than 34% of homosexual men freely expressed regret at being homosexual. Possibly more than this proportion felt regret but did not express it. 17% had 'considered giving up being gay' and 9% would 'take a pill today' to make them heterosexual (if one were available).

* The above is an extract from *Homosexuality – The Medical, Social and Religious Implications*, produced by The Maranatha Community. See page 41 for address details.

© *The Maranatha Community June, 1997*

Disabled and homosexual

Information from the Association to Aid the Sexual and Personal Relationships of People with a Disability (SPOD)

Why this article needs to be written:

A man telephoned SPOD in great distress. 'How dare they assume I am heterosexual', he finally blurted out. Middle-aged and suffering from MS he had been admitted to residential care. The home was quite progressive about relationships, allowing partners to stay for nights or weekends. However, as the caller put it, 'the whole place seems to be run on heterosexual innuendo – mostly generated by the staff'. The caller had been in a relationship for fourteen years and would have liked his partner to stay with him on the same terms as the partners of other residents . . .

At the time of writing (1993) it is considered at a conservative estimate that 10% of the population

is predominantly homosexual. Therefore it would seem to follow that 10% of people with disabilities are likely to be homosexual too. Yet the number of homosexual men and women who contact SPOD is less than 1%. Perhaps this is because SPOD has not always made it clear that the Association is for everyone with a disability, irrespective of their sexual orientation.

By definition, a short article like this has to resort to generalities. Basically its purpose is to be consciousness-raising for both the man and the woman with a disability who think they may be homosexual and for carers to realise that not everyone with a disability is heterosexual.

Homosexuality is as natural and normal for some people as heterosexuality is for others.

Because the issues are different for men who are homosexual from women who are homosexual, they are looked at separately. People in the two groups like to be referred to as gay men and lesbians and they are referred to subsequently as such.

Lesbian women

For a lesbian with a disability the first problem may be in getting information about her sexuality. Most sex education does not mention lesbianism. The media, heterosexual friends and family may be full of prejudice and misinformation. If one in ten women is lesbian, statistically almost everyone is likely to have someone in their family or social circle who is lesbian. Many have been persuaded consciously or unconsciously to suppress their lesbianism and try to be heterosexual. Many lesbians are married with families and it is not unusual for women to reach 40, 60 or 70 before realising their own sexual identity. In an often homophobic culture feeling confident about your sexual orientation is important.

It is important to think about the lifestyle that would best suit the individual – to have several partners or to have one or to have none; to have short or long-term relationships. How a woman expresses her lesbianism is very individual and personal. It is important to learn to feel happy with one's own body. Masturbation and self-pleasure are valuable ways to learn about your body and what pleases you sexually. Many women have never had adequate information about their own sexual potential.

Lovers can caress each other simultaneously or singly, with hands or mouth. If there is no sensation in the genital area, remember any part of your body can be a sensual area. If your partner can orgasm you can share in her pleasure. Because both partners are women it doesn't mean they are carbon copies. Many find intense enjoyment in breast stimulation, others like vaginal penetration, whilst others find earlobes, neck, back, buttocks, inner thighs, feet, palms, particularly pleasing. Special sensitive massage before or after sharing sex can extend the closeness. Remember, the clitoris is the only organ of a woman's body solely for pleasure. Stimulation can be by the fingers or by the side of the hand or with a sex aid if you find this more convenient.

Gay men

Until 1967 when the Homosexual Reform Act was passed, it was against the law for two men to indulge in

sexual activity together. The 1967 Act made it legal for two consenting males over the age of 21 to have a homosexual relationship in private. It should be noted that the age of consent for heterosexuals is 16 and that 'in private' is open to debate, as an hotel or residential home can be deemed to be a public place.

Gay men today are indistinguishable from heterosexual men and will often have the same concerns about health, diet, staying young looking and keeping fit. For a man who is homosexual and disabled, these expectations can be daunting. Like his lesbian counterpart a gay man may have had difficulty getting information about his sexuality. Most sex education does not mention homosexuality. The media, heterosexual friends and family may be full of prejudices and misinformation, that gay men are bad, miserable, AID's carriers and child molesters whose only expression of sexuality is sodomy. Assuming that if one in ten men is homosexual and many more will indulge in homosexual activity from time to time, again statistically everyone is likely to have someone in their family or social circle who is homosexual.

Although men's sexuality tends to be focused on the penis, gay men's

sexuality is usually far from the common image of sodomy. Many men will have explored other erogenous zones as well as mutual masturbation and oral sex. HIV/AID's has made most men more careful and practise safer sex, but intercourse even using a condom is not 100% safe but only as safe as the condom user.

This article is from a series of resource and information leaflets for both the person with a disability and/or their partner and for professional workers. The leaflets are intended to be informative and thought-provoking. They can also be used as a starting-point and permission giving.

Further or more detailed information can be obtained by writing to or telephoning the SPOD office.

SPOD provides
- Counselling by telephone or in a client's home area if possible and where appropriate.

- An information and advice service.

- Education and training on the sexual aspects of disability.

© Information from The Association to Aid the Sexual and Personal Relationships of People with a Disability (SPOD)

Young gay men talking

School – the best days of your life?

Kevin: 'Occasionally the teacher would bring up the idea of homosexuality and being gay and then it was such an amazement to the rest of the class because no one else would bring it up. And then some sort of really ignorant remarks would come from the boys, the lads at the back of the class.'

Daniel: 'The only mention of gay men was jokes. Even the teachers made jokes at my expense because of the rumours about me. Which is something I found really hurtful.'

Andy: 'I'd say don't tell a school friend first unless they're the closest, closest, closest most trustworthy friend you know. One of the people I told let slip and suddenly the whole year knew. Nobody said anything directly to me but I did notice a lot of the boys suddenly weren't friends and they'd ignore me and they'd sort of be laughing when I was around. Other people I know have had a much worse time than that, but it was bad enough.'

Many of us hoped that we'd get information about being attracted to men in sex education classes.

Kevin: 'It's funny now because at the time I thought I was the only one, and yet now I see four of us out at the gay club I go to. From the year below there's about another four that I see around.'

Tim: 'I was waiting and expecting to hear something about homosexuality, safe sex and different things in sex education. Maybe some information that could help me. But I got nothing. There was nothing.'

It may be hard to believe, but there are probably other people at school who are having the same sorts of feelings as you. Perhaps also like you, they are frightened of saying anything. (Other people do not begin to wonder whether they're gay or not until they've left school. That's quite normal too!)

Kevin: 'I wish that my friends had known a lot more than they did. A lot of them – the girls – they didn't really care. And that was fine for them. But a lot of my, what were my best friends, just clammed. So for my last few months at school I would always sit with the girls. Lunchtimes I never used to spend in the classroom because no one understood. That was the only thing that was hard to come to terms with. Everyone's reaction to it. Like all my friends at school, they used to come and stay round mine. Ben used to sleep on my bedroom floor, and all that just sort of stopped, and we stopped doing everything together and it all just went. That was the only hard thing – why didn't they understand? Why was it so alien to them?

'Ben couldn't understand it because we'd done holidays together and I would act as one of the lads. Like in the pub – we'd drink loads and I think it was just so hard for him. I don't think he could cope with me sort of going from being one of the lads to saying, "He's nice" when I was having a laugh with the girls.

'I think you need to . . . perhaps even not tell your school friends. Try to lead a double life for a while. And just sort of see if you find new friends before you just dump everything and say, that's it. Because I think it's a lot easier to be gay if your school friends put two and two together, without you just telling them, and them reacting harshly. Because I think they accept it a lot easier than if you just smack them in the fact with it.'

• The above is an extract from *Young Gay Men Talking*, produced by AVERT. See page 41 for address details. ©*AVERT*

Christianity and homosexuality

A short introduction

Homosexuality and the Church

Most Christians have believed and most churches have taught that you cannot be a Christian and express you love for another person of the same sex in a sexual relationship. They believe that God has condemned this through the Bible.

We must remind ourselves of the world the people of the Bible actually lived in. Life was hard and survival was a nation's concern. Today, in the West, we may find it hard to comprehend the emphasis placed on child-bearing in ancient societies. In biblical times people were faced every day with basic threats to their individual and communal survival. Therefore, forms of sexuality which seemed to be at odds with the institution of the family were rejected and condemned. The law of the Jews in Christ's time illustrated this general pattern, though in other aspects it represented for its day a more careful and merciful code than the traditions of neighbouring peoples.

Christianity began as a Jewish sect; Christ was a Jew and so were all his apostles. Though the new Christian faith replaced the old Jewish law in the eyes of the early Christians, both are intimately and inextricably linked. Ancient fears about homosexuality were deeply founded in the consciousness of early Christians, whether Jewish or not, and Christianity itself certainly did not remove them.

The story of Sodom and Gomorrah is often quoted; but the real point of it is an understandable condemnation of what amounts to gang rape. It is not a condemnation of homosexual relationships as we would understand them today. It is significant that when Jesus used the story of Sodom he said that the people of that city would find the Day of

The logo of the Movement combines three symbols:

The **Lambda** is the Greek letter 'L' and is the first letter of the word 'liberation'; it has long been the international sign for gay liberation. **The Cross**: The central symbol of the Christian faith. **The Circle**: the symbol of that wholeness and completion towards which we strive and yearn through our living our relationships.

Judgement easier to bear than those who refused to welcome his disciples and give them hospitality (Luke 10:11-12). And whenever else the destruction of Sodom and Gomorrah is referred to in the Bible, homosexuality isn't even mentioned.

Paul in his letters condemned the practice of heterosexual men having intercourse with male prostitutes in pagan temples. He thought this idolatrous because human beings were used as objects of worship rather than honour being given to God. It was all destructive of love, and Paul then showed how Christ's power can rescue us from such a pattern of life if we commit ourselves to him in trust. God wants us, through Jesus, to love one another as he loved us (John 13:34).

In many respects the Church was limited by the social outlook of the times and places where the Gospel was preached. Attitudes have always changed, however slowly. Only in the last century was slavery abolished, but Paul accepted it without question. And it is only in recent times that the churches have started to examine the position of women in their own organisations and in society in general. The time is now right to have a critical look at homosexuality in a Christian context.

The Lesbian & Gay Christian Movement is not selling out on Christian truth. It is working for the very love and freedom that Christ brings to his people through his life, death and resurrection. Our Movement is working for love, for peace, for justice, and for the promotion of the Christian faith. God's work is always a struggle. Let us try to be at the heart of it.

Homosexuality today

You may gave heard that somebody in your family or among your friends or at work is homosexual. Maybe it was just a whisper at a family gathering or in the canteen. Perhaps you were surprised. You might be even more astonished if the person concerned had actually told you face to face – and that is happening quite often these days.

More and more lesbian and gay people are proud to be out!

Our sexuality has far more to do with the kind of people we are and how we love others than it has to do with what happens in bed. We are no more responsible or irresponsible than anyone else. Sexual orientation has been described as 'an innocent accident'. And yet there are sections of society and the Church which either refuse to acknowledge lesbian and gay people or (perhaps worse) ignore them. Both of these attitudes are based on prejudice or lack of information, or both. Few people stop to think what it's like to be homosexual. Have you ever asked a new acquaintance 'are you married?' and received the answer, 'No I'm gay'? Are you aware that a quarter of a million homosexuals died in Hitler's concentration camps because they were gay – and that many who survived received no compensation after the War? Do you know enough to understand homosexuality?

Do you know any homosexuals?

If you think you don't, you're mistaken – their numbers are such that most people know many lesbian and gay people without realising what their sexual orientation is, and of course they include members of your family and married people.

What is homosexuality?

A crime? – Not any longer in the UK as long as you are over 18 (if you're male), aren't in the services or the merchant navy, don't live on the Isle of Man or Channel Isles, and do it in total privacy. Lesbians have never figured in the law of these islands.

A disease? – No, it's not, and you can't catch it either! Homosexuals do not need medical advice any more than heterosexuals do.

A homosexual is indeed a person who is attracted physically to another of the same sex. You may believe that sex has no other dimension than producing children. But if you move beyond this narrow vision of sex, you will know that it can give a richness and a depth to relationships which are founded on love. So a lesbian or gay man is not only a sexual being, but someone seeking to give love as well as receive it.

Our understanding of many things has changed and our understanding of sex is changing too.

The Lesbian & Gay Christian Movement needs and wants to be in the vanguard of these changes.

Some facts about homosexuality

Homosexuality is unusual but not unnatural. You could draw a parallel with being left-handed. A hundred years ago you would have been forced to be right-handed, but today it isn't a cause of active discrimination against you. And about one person in ten is predominantly homosexual in orientation. There are many more gay people in Britain than the whole population of Wales.

There is no real evidence to suggest that homosexuality is caused by emotional trauma, or a possessive mother, or an absent father. Some psychiatrists claim that all their homosexual patients are neurotic, but so are their heterosexual patients! Why else are they too on the couch?

High-minded moralists ask for strict laws to protect the young from homosexuals. But no greater proportion of homosexual men and women molest young children than do heterosexuals. The number is small. Some think that young people can be made into homosexuals, but no reputable psychiatrist would agree with this. What is more often needed is a friend or a counsellor to help a person clear away confusion about his or her sexual orientation. This can prevent the years of suffering and agony that people may otherwise have to endure before accepting the truth about themselves.

Can homosexuality be 'cured' or 'corrected'?

Young people who show 'homosexual tendencies' are often advised to get married and have a family; all will then be well, they are told. But these 'cure' marriages rarely, if ever, work and they often end in tragedy, especially for the heterosexual partner and the children. A person needs to be sure that his or her homosexual behaviour is only very superficial before even thinking of marriage.

Rather, such young people need to be supported and respected in the process of trying to work through their doubts and insecurities about themselves. Without such acceptance and understanding, they may feel so threatened as to undergo extreme 'therapies', or to be 'exorcised' by misguided, albeit well-intentioned, Christians. This may temporarily change their behaviour, but dangerously blocks the facing of uncertainty which alone can lead to self-acceptance and the encouragement of responsible decisions about themselves. [These organisations are often called 'ex-gay', but frequently avoid these term in the fact of critical publicity.]

Statement of conviction

It is the conviction of the members of the Lesbian & Gay Christian Movement that human sexuality in all its richness is a gift of God gladly to be accepted, enjoyed and honoured as a way of both expressing and growing in love, in accordance with the life and teaching of Jesus Christ. Therefore it is their conviction that it is entirely compatible with the Christian faith not only to love another person of the same sex but also to express that love fully in a personal sexual relationship.

© Lesbian & Gay Christian Movement (LGCM)

Faith, hope and homosexuality

The witness of Scripture

General points

The Bible was written over many centuries in several cultures – all of them different from our own. But this does not invalidate the abiding authority of scriptural revelation. We see no reason why God should not make particular expressions of his will within these cultures the expression of his permanent will for all cultures. In any case, the Bible stands frequently over against contemporary culture. Both Jesus and Paul are often diametrically opposed to social convention – on moral as well as spiritual matters (Mark 2:23-8; 7:1-8; John 7:53-8; Acts 19:23-41; Gal. 1:11-17). That they are in agreement with their cultures at other points does not invalidate this basic critical integrity.

Having said this, it must be acknowledged that direct references to homosexuality in Scripture are relatively few. Even so, they belong to a much broader context of biblical teaching on creation, love, holiness and human relationships – teaching which goes to the heart of God's purpose for humankind. We shall deal with this broader context first, and then discuss those texts which refer more specifically to homosexual practice.

When God created the first man and woman, he was well satisfied with his handiwork: it was 'very good' (Gen. 1:31). The early chapters of Genesis do not go into great detail about the distinctions between female and male – but they do emphasise that each was a separate, intentional creation, and that they were made to be complementary rather than 'two of the same'. It is these chapters which provide the basic context for human sexuality, procreation and marriage (Gen. 1:27-8; 2:18-24). They are foundational for the Judaeo-Christian teaching

that sexual intercourse is designed for expression solely within the life-long, marital relationship of a man and a woman.[1]

Of course, biblical models of sex, marriage and reproduction must be related in turn to the essential quality of love. The concept of love in the Bible extends far beyond sexual love. God's love defines our love, not the other way round: 'We love because he first loved us' (1 Jn. 4:19). God himself is Trinity – a community of persons in perfect loving relationship.

These principles are relevant to every area of our lives. They bear vitally on all our loving, and not least on our sexual loving. God's creation of the human race extends his love outwards and opens the way to a covenant of mutual trust and care. When God saw that it was not good for Adam to be alone, he created an 'other' – a woman – to be his companion (Gen. 2:20-5). The complementarity of woman and man is both physical and relational. They are designed anatomically for one other: they correspond genitally and procreatively in a way two men (or two women) do not. We are aware that this point has been dismissed as a 'naturalistic fallacy' – a leap of logic from 'what is' to 'what has been intended' or 'what ought to be'.[2] We

also recognise that heterosexual sex is hardly confined to penile-vaginal penetration and reproduction. Even so, the link between heterosexual activity and procreation is more than incidental. Granted, the vast majority of such activity is not finally procreative; granted, God gave us sex for pleasure, too; granted, large numbers of men and women, who for whatever reason cannot produce children, continue to enjoy sex. Still, there can be no doubt that Scripture takes the procreative capacity of heterosexual activity to be a mark of its exclusive divine endorsement – something which validates it over against other, inherently 'sterile' forms of shared sexual practice (Gen. 1:28; 9:1-15; 15:1-21; Ps. 127:3).[3]

Of course, the complementarity of woman and man is more than physical. Genesis 1:27 emphasises that God created human beings in his own image – male and female together. The context shows that this divine image is expressed in a relationship which may be physical, but which is also spiritual, emotional and psychological. Man and woman are equally human (insofar as they have the same nature), but are nonetheless qualitatively different and complementary. Their being joined together as husband and wife becomes a fundamental expression of all this: 'So a man will leave his father and his mother and be united with his wife, and they will become one flesh' (Gen. 2:24). Here is the definitive pattern for human sexual love. We accept that this pattern was not immediately confined to monogamous marriage in the Old Testament, but would stress that monogamy emerged from it as its purposed end. Certainly, it is applied to monogamous marriage by both Jesus and Paul (Matt. 19:4-6; Eph. 5:31).[4]

It is clear, then, that biblical Christian teaching on sexual love would see it expressed properly in the lifelong relationship of one man and one woman in marriage. What is more, the Bible warns severely against disregarding this teaching, and hedges it round with laws and obligations designed to reinforce its status (Matt. 19:4-12; 1 Cor. 7:1-40; Col. 3:18-19; Tit. 2:4-5; 1 Pet. 3:1-7; Heb. 13:4). Indeed, the duties attendant upon husband and wife exemplify a principle which is often overlooked in gay and lesbian exegesis – namely that obedience to God's commands is not to be set over against Christ's rule of love; rather, such obedience is itself a mark of that love (Jn. 15:10; 1 Jn 5:2-4).

While so much current debate centres on sexual activity, we should reiterate the key place in God's purposes of other forms of non-erotic love – e.g. sisterly and brotherly love (*philadelphia*), and love expressed in friendship (*philia*). A classic example which illustrates both is that of David and Jonathan. Nor should we forget that Jesus chose friends whom he regarded as 'family' (Mark 3:33-5). The closest of these were Peter, James and John, the latter of whom was distinguished as 'the disciple whom Jesus loved' (Jn. 21:20). These examples confirm that we need not be fearful of same-sex friendships. They should also spur us to reject insinuations that such friendships must involve homosexual activity. It has become a staple of pro-gay exegesis, for example, to present David and Jonathan in homoerotic terms – even though the text offers no credible evidence of this.[5]

Christians should be the first to insist that there are valid and honourable forms of love outside of marriage. Friendship between people of the same sex has been not only acknowledged, but acclaimed throughout the Church's history. The dilemma today is that contemporary attitudes make it increasingly difficult for such forms of love to exist without suspicion. This is much to be regretted.

It is important to note in this context that many homosexual people, for Christian or other reasons, are committed to chastity – that is, to abstention from genital sex. In this, they resemble many heterosexuals (whether single, divorced or widowed) who believe it right to refrain from genital sex – however much they may long for the full, physical sexual relationship offered by marriage (cf. 1 Cor. 7:11; 1 Tim. 5:9). In addition, of course, there are those of both orientations who have chosen the equally hard way of celibacy – that is, a lifelong, rather than a provisional, commit-ment to sexual abstinence. Not only did Jesus himself live a single celibate life; he seems to have recognised and commended others who observed this pattern, even making a distinction between those (probably impotent but possibly with a strong same-sex orientation), who had been 'born' to observe it, those (probably castrated courtiers, but possibly others) who had been 'made that way by people', and those called to renounce marriage 'because of the kingdom of heaven' (cf. 1 Cor. 7:7).

Sources:

1   For an exposition of this see T.E. Schmidt, *Straight and Narrow?*, pp. 39-63.
2   For a summary of this critique see Vasey, M., *Strangers and Friends*, pp. 48ff.
3   For an elaboration of this argument see Hilborn, D., 'For the Procreation of Children', in Durber, S. (ed.), *As Man and Woman Made: Theological Reflections on Marriage*, London: The United Reformed Church, 1994, pp. 22-32.
4   Cf. Vasey, M., *Strangers and Friends*, pp. 115-8.
5   1 Sam. 18:1-2 Sam 1:26. Cf Vasey, M. *Strangers and Friends*, pp. 120-1, and Halperin, D., *One Hundred Years of Homosexuality*, London, Routledge, 1990, Ch.4. But even Greenberg, who is usually more even-handed on such matters, resorts to speculating and arguing from silence on this point. He begins by admitting, 'In neither case does the text mention a sexual aspect to the relationship'. Yet then he goes on to surmise that 'an explicit homosexual relationship could easily have been deleted by priestly editors . . .'. So, for that matter, could much else which we should like to be in Scripture, but which does not appear there! Greenberg, D.F., *The Construction of Homosexuality*, pp. 113-4.

• The above is an extract from *Faith, Hope & Homosexuality*, produced by the Evangelical Alliance's Commission on Unity and Truth among Evangelicals (ACUTE). See page 41 for address details.

© Evangelical Alliance

Private lives

After divorcing, you came out as gay. How do you now tell your children about your new partner?

The problem

'I am a gay man of 40, who has been in a stable, loving relationship for over a year. I was married for 15 years until two years ago and I have two girls, aged 14 and 12, and a boy of five. I married to satisfy family pressure to "do the right thing", smothering the knowledge that I was gay. My problem is, how do I tell my children about my partner? The girls are aware I am gay; the elder girl and I have a good relationship, but the younger one has asked me not to write or call as it upsets her. My boy knows nothing, but at what age and how can the subject be introduced? My ex-wife veers between wishing us well and vindictive bitterness. I'm convinced she has tried to poison the girls towards me and is obstructive about access to my son. But I feel I can no longer conceal from them the fact that I have a partner.'

Give them time

As the daughter of a man who 'came out' after my parents' divorce, I sympathise with your situation. My feeling at first was shock. I thought: what if my father had come out all those years ago and I had never existed? I suspect this is what upsets your younger daughter. If that is so, it will pass.

Your ex may well be saying things to the children, but that would not give you the right to use them as pawns against her. I was left feeling piggy-in-the-middle for many years when my parents stopped speaking. Do not let this happen to your elder daughter; it will only make things worse and she will resent one or both of you. The only people she needs to talk to about your new relationship are her sister, you and, when the time comes, her brother.

Do talk to her, but listen, too. There will be tears, but it will help, and if she and your other children come out of it knowing they were not to blame for the split, then you will have saved a lot of heartache. Be honest without being explicit and remember that all step-parents, be they gay, straight or bi, are a potential threat to children caught up in divorces. They may accept that you are gay without being ready to spend a lot of time with your partner, regardless of what he is like as a person, or the fact that he is male.

When to tell your son only you can decide, but please don't put too much pressure on them too quickly. They will all need their own time to accept that you have a partner who is not their mother, male or otherwise.

You probably feel on top of the world now you have accepted yourself and found a man you are happy with, but your children will still feel pain over the divorce and may do so for a long time to come. But, like me, they may forge a new, stronger relationship with their father.

DB, London

Back off

I am a gay man of 52, with a lover of nine years' standing. I can understand the pressures you have been through, but I think you are being a greedy wimp.

You say you always knew you were gay but that you succumbed to the many family pressures that make people conform to a stereotype of a heterosexual relationship. You had three children – why didn't you stop at one, if you had to prove your heterosexuality, fecundity and conformity?

You are probably naïve, in a gay sense, if you think that a relationship of only one year's standing can be classified as stable and loving. You make no mention of the history or age of your partner or how he feels about your dilemma. Could he cope with closer contact with your children, who might represent to him a very palpable denial of the sexuality you share with him?

Your wife should be your main

source of concern. You have to understand her bitterness towards you. I can. Every day she will be thinking of what you get up to in bed with another man. She will hate to think of that. She has care of your children and as one of your girls approaches a sexually active life herself, she cannot help but regard you as, at best, no help to her at a difficult time, at worst, as someone who complicates the sexual and family patterns she wants to put across to your children. She may be especially worried that you will try to portray to your son a vision of your new life that implies that what you have done is very common.

You have an instinct to want to parade your new life. You shouldn't do it. A lot of 'straight' men who 'go gay' at your age make this big mistake. You won't love me for telling you that, in gay circles, it's well-known that men with your background almost always find themselves the weaker male in the new partnership: passive emotionally and passive sexually. You need time to sort out your homosexuality before you revisit the heterosexuality of your past life.

You say you want your children to know about your partner. Does he want to know about them? Do they want to know about him? I doubt it. In the triangle you have created, you are the odd angle. Accept that you have destroyed your first life. Maybe your children will refind you. You should leave that up to them to do, as they mature. Maybe they will, maybe they won't. If they have a stable and happy upbringing, it's likely that they will want to fit you back into their lives, but at their pace and on their terms.

You sound to me, a gay man who has never fathered children, like someone who wants it all. You can't have it. Back off and get on with your new life.

Robert Forsythe, Norfolk
© The Guardian
November, 1997

Synod decides to take a fresh look at old attitudes

By Kathy Marks

The Church of England last night confronted the issue of homosexual priests for the first time in a decade, in a highly charged General Synod debate that exposed the gulf dividing Anglicans.

Both liberal and traditionalist speakers at the meeting in York warned that the issue could provoke a mass exodus from the Church. The Archbishop of Canterbury, Dr George Carey, poured cold water on gay Christians' hopes for a more liberal approach, saying he did not 'share the assumption that it is only a matter of time before the Church will change its mind'.

The debate was prompted by a motion tabled by the Archdeacon of Wandsworth, the Ven David Gerrard, asking Synod to acknowledge that a document issued by bishops in 1991 was 'not the last word on the subject'. The document stated that while practising gays could take their place as lay members of the Church, they were not welcome among the ranks of clergy.

In a moving speech, the Rev Michael Vasey, a theology lecturer who has argued that homosexual acts are not forbidden by the Bible, denounced the Church as hostile to gay Christians. He said that his evangelical opponents had made two attempts to 'out' him. 'In the first attempt, three people who are now diocesan bishops in this room were silent partners,' he said. 'The Church is a place of danger for gay people. That is why we are leaving in droves . . . '

'So often the Church has failed to lead in preventing or rectifying injustice. Indeed, some of our past and present teaching may give some twisted and prejudiced people justification for their violent persecutions of gay people, however much we may deplore such actions.'

Mr Gerrard asked delegates: 'Is mere condemnation of homophobia sufficient while homosexuals, both lay and clergy, have often only been accepted in our churches if they have been prepared to remain invisible and inaudible?'

The Rev Malcolm Johnson, from London, added: 'I find it obscene that happily married heterosexual bishops condemn their gay clergy to celibacy. I believe we need an ethic for homosexuals other than "stop it".'

In response, Canon Max Wigley, from Bradford, said any modification of the Church's stance would be damaging. He said: 'If ever legislation is passed by this Synod which allows for practising homosexuals to be ordained, I am afraid that the number of clergy and lay people who will leave the Church of England will make the numbers who left over the ordination of women look infinitesimal.' He was backed by Alison Ruoff, a lay delegate from Hertfordshire, who said the Scriptures made clear that homosexual acts were unnatural and therefore wrong. 'Homosexuals are not born as such: the choice to go on sinning is theirs,' she said.

Dr Carey pleased hardliners by expressing uncompromising opposition to homosexual acts. 'I do not find any justification, from the Bible or the entire Christian tradition, for sexual activity outside marriage,' he said. 'Thus same-sex relationships in my view cannot be on a par with marriage. Clergy, especially, must model relationships that commend the faith of Christ.'

© The Independent
July, 1997

Gay pair insist on right to 'family child'

Martin Wainwright on a couple advertising for a woman to deliver them the child they are not allowed to foster or adopt

Two gay men are seeking a surrogate mother for a 'family child', it emerged yesterday, hours after the Government announced tentative plans for a review of the law.

The couple from Greater Manchester, who say they have 'a God-given right to be parents', are looking for a mother or a lesbian couple who would have a child by artificial insemination and share his or her upbringing.

'I know that we would be brilliant parents,' said Russell Conlon, aged 39, a former stonemason whose efforts to adopt or foster have been refused on disability grounds. He has osteoarthritis and the brittle-bone disease osteoporosis while his partner Chris Joyce, 32, is epileptic.

The two men, who are unemployed and live in Collyhurst on the edge of Manchester, are using gay contacts and searching magazine classified ads for a potential mother in a settled relationship. There is nothing in law to prevent a surrogacy provided financial inducements are not offered, although the arrangement has no legal force and the mother could change her mind at any time about bearing the child, or about plans for its future.

'I have wanted children all my life and now I've found the right person, I want to go ahead,' said Mr Joyce, who has known Mr Conlon for 12 years but began a sexual relationship only last August. Mr Conlon said: 'We are deeply committed to one another and we had a blessing last December which we consider as strong as marriage. We love each other very much and in the eyes of God we are married.'

> **'This may be a mutually beneficial arrangement for the men, but it wouldn't be beneficial for the child to be brought up in such a strange situation'**

Both men work for a gay support network in Manchester called Happy Families. They said their decision was influenced by getting to know other gay people with children, who led happy and normal family lives.

'We are prepared to do anything for a child,' Mr Conlon said. 'We feel that the love and respect which a child brings would complete our lives. We all have a right to have children. It doesn't matter who or what we are. I want to be able to partake in that right.'

The Confederation of Health Authorities called for clearer guidelines on surrogacy, however, particularly in cases where GPs could face 'extraordinarily difficult moral decisions' in advising their patients. Stephen Thornton, of the confederation, said the Manchester couple formed a 'classic case' of a dilemma that needed to be clarified nationally.

The case adds to the pressure on the health minister Tessa Jowell to agree a wide-ranging review of surrogacy, which is being examined

by her department in the light of the Karen Roche case. Mrs Roche, a mother from Scarborough, pulled out of a surrogacy arrangement with a Dutch couple.

The Department of Health said yesterday the report on the Roche case would consider financial arrangements which might breach the 1995 law which banned commercial surrogacy. The Dutch couple are understood to have offered £12,000 in expenses plus clothes and travel, and there is widespread scepticism about how practical private, unpaid arrangements are beyond people who already know one another.

Mr Conlon said he and Mr Joyce were prepared to pay expenses to a potential mother, even though both are on benefits. The couple are still attempting to adopt or foster, in spite of the refusal from Manchester social services, and are due for further medical tests after taking advice from a solicitor.

Mr Joyce would be the donor if surrogacy went ahead as Mr Conlon is unable to have children. Mr Conlon said: 'I just want to be able to hear someone call me "Dad" and I will fight all the way for it.'

The proposal was strongly criticised by Nicholas Winterton, Tory MP for Macclesfield, who said the needs of the child were overlooked. 'This may be a mutually beneficial arrangement for the men, but it wouldn't be beneficial for the child to be brought up in such a strange situation. I don't want to harass those who have a different leaning, but children should not be subjected to this abnormality.'

Mr Winterton added: 'I hope that society will decide that it is wrong that children and babies should become pawns in the need for individuals to gratify their emotions.'

The Rev Ian Brown, vicar of Halliwell, near Bolton, said: 'This is the wrong environment in which to bring up children. It must be very confusing to have two mums and two dads.'

'I know that we would be brilliant parents. We love each other very much and in the eyes of God we are married.'
Russell Conlon

The arguments

For

Linda Bellos, lesbian activist, former council leader:
'I feel exactly the same about surrogacy for gay and lesbian couples as I do about heterosexual couples: a bit iffy. Whether they're gay or heterosexual is irrelevant. The argument that a lesbian or gay couple will make bad parents is utter rubbish. Those who make active choices to be parents often make very good parents: those children are desired, rather than the fruit of desire.

'Some see being a parent as a right, others believe they have to do it in order to be seen as a complete woman, or even a complete family. But families take different forms. Among the lesbian and gay communities families express their strengths in different ways.

'One of the arguments against lesbian or gay parenting is that we will abuse our children. But a far smaller proportion of abuse goes on in lesbian and gay households. Abuse is about power.'

Against

Baroness Warnock, moral philosopher:
'It may be extremely dangerous to go down the road of making this acceptable. It's a question of who they get, related to the question of payment. Most people would want a substantial amount of money.

'It's all very well to be liberal about artificial insemination by donor but surrogacy is a totally different thing. The whole thing of carrying a child for nine months makes it a different business.

'I don't think there's any problem inherent in a gay couple bringing up a child, but any surrogacy arrangement is problematic.

'I can easily foresee an extra dimension of difficulty in the question of who is the biological father. For one or other it might be a biological child – the other one might become jealous. And what if they split up? I suspect that if you decide to live with a homosexual partner you've got to forgo bringing up a child. It's not a right.'
© *The Guardian*
May, 1997

'I have wanted children all my life and now I've found the right person.'
Chris Joyce

'This is the wrong environment in which to bring up children.'
The Rev Ian Brown

'I hope that society will decide that it is wrong that children and babies should become pawns in the need for individuals to gratify their emotions.'
Nicholas Winterton MP
© *The Guardian*
May, 1997

Personal stories

Sex education

Steven (21-30)

I came out at the age of 13, whilst at comprehensive school. It caused rather a commotion at the time. There were meetings with my headmaster, social services, the police, probation service, my parents and sometimes even me! Although in retrospect they all seemed to be struggling somewhat with my situation, in that first month they all said they were there to help me. I never saw them again. During the next three and a half years I was subjected to continual bullying from other pupils, often ending up in physical violence. Although each recorded incident of violence was dealt with by the teachers, the root cause was never addressed. Unfortunately, I feel nothing has changed since them.

Michael (17)

I am 17 years old and gay. It is wrong that others should look down on gays. I have been beaten by other guys (queer bashing). I know other guys 16 to 20 that are gay and are afraid to tell anyone. One of my friends committed suicide at 18 because of being bullied.

Anonymous (21)

I had a very sheltered, but happy, childhood in a very small town in the north of England. I had no idea what a homosexual was, and when I had my first homosexual experience, I was more than confused and had no one to talk to. I have not become any different in my adult life. I am not a confused, screwed-up 20-something basket case. But I do know people who are. I admitted to myself that I was homosexual at around 15 years old. But if I had known that there were other people like me it would have made things a lot easier.

Jon (21)

I was very unhappy at school and was bullied as people suspected that I was gay. The only time that gay people were mentioned in sex education was when someone asked why I was a poof. The biology teacher explained that people were poofs because they were missing a chromosome – very helpful! I feel that the fear that I lived in at school took a heavy toll in terms of my educational achievements and also psychological development. Happily I am now a well-adjusted person and am not frightened to be who I am.

Stuart (21)

Without support from an early age, or understanding from the world around me, my early life as a young homosexual was confused, difficult and largely unfulfilled. I feel that if the age of consent was lowered, more support groups and a better understanding would prevail, making the life of young homosexuals much happier, more fulfilling and more stable.

Claire (21)

As someone just about to enter the teaching profession I am extremely concerned about the lack of inclusive sex education. I come from a very open family and had reasonable sex education at school, but from a totally heterosexual viewpoint with maybe a couple of mentions of the fact that

10% of the population is gay. I feel that the lack of discussion of gay sex meant that I did not feel able to say I was bisexual until I was 21, while I had heterosexual sex at age 15. For me it was good to discover another side to myself and make sense of my infatuations with certain women, but for someone who feels exclusively gay those years must be a frightening time.

Anonymous (31)

Sex education was 'straight' sex only. Our headmaster made it clear during assembly that any sex between boys that was discovered would be treated by calling the police, the boys' parents and a psychiatrist and the boy would be 'cured'. Looking back I think I would be classified as clinically depressed between the ages of 12-17 as I felt my sexuality was a psychiatric problem and a secret. If I had been told that homosexuality was another variation that was OK then I'm sure I would have developed as a person in a more balanced way.

Jason (21)

In sex education class the teacher looked round the room and said that as there weren't any homosexuals in the class (actual words: 'nobody looks homosexual') there was no need to discuss it!!

Amanda (21)

My sex education consisted of being shown various forms of contraception and being told how these were used. There was no discussion of the emotional side of sex and sexuality (for any sexuality).

• The above is an extract from *Arrested development?*, a survey produced by Stonewall. See page 41 for address details.

© Stonewall

ADDITIONAL RESOURCES

You might like to contact the following organisations for further information. Due to the increasing cost of postage, many organisations cannot respond to enquiries unless they receive a stamped, addressed envelope.

AIDS Education and Research Trust (AVERT)
11-13 Denne Parade
Horsham
West Sussex
RH12 1JD
Tel: 01403 210202
Fax: 01403 211001
Web site: see page 43 for details
Works to prevent people becoming infected with HIV and dying from Aids through education and research. Works with others to develop a cure. Publishes a wide range of educational booklets. Ask for their Resources Catalogue.

Amnesty International United Kingdom (AIUK)
99-119 Roseberry Avenue
London
EC1R 4RE
Tel: 0171 814 6200
Fax: 0171 833 1510
Campaigns within Britain about their worldwide concerns. Amnesty International is a worldwide human rights movement which is independent of any government, political faction, ideology, economic interest of religious creed.

Association to Aid the Sexual and Personal Relationships of People with a Disability (SPOD)
286 Camden Road
London
N7 0BJ
Tel: 0171 607 8851
Srimulates public and professional awareness of sexual needs and difficulties among disabled people. Offers advice, counselling and information organisation; produces leaflets, resource lists, information and books.

Evangelical Alliance
Whitefield House
186 Kennington Park Road
London
SE11 4BT
Tel: 0171 207 2100
Fax: 0171 207 2150
The Evangelical Alliance's Commission on Unity and Truth among Evangelicals (ACUTE), produces the publication *Faith, Hope & Homosexuality*.

Lesbian & Gay Christian Movement (LGCM)
Oxford House
Derbyshire Street
London
E2 6HG
Tel: 0171 739 1249
Fax: 0171 739 1249
Offers gay liberation to the churches and Crhist to the gay community. Produces publications.

Maranatha Community
102 Irlam Street
Flixton
Manchester
M41 6JT
Tel: 0161 748 4858
Fax: 0161 747 7379
The Maranatha Community is a Christian movement which involves members of many different strands within the Christian faith. Their central aim is to become more effective Christians in life, work and worship. Produces publications.

Stonewall Lobby Group Ltd
2 Greycoat Place
London
SW1P 1SB
Tel: 0171 222 9007
Fax: 0171 222 0525
Web site: See page 41 for details
Works to achieve fully equal legal rights for lesbians and gay men in the UK, by providing information and support for legislators. Produces publications.

Terrence Higgins Trust
52-54 Gray's Inn Road
London
WC1X 8JU
Tel: 0171 831 0330
Fax: 0171 242 0121
Promotes understanding of HIV and AIDS issues by collecting and disseminating medical and social information. Produces information on HIV and AIDS and general information for homosexual men.

War on Want
37-39 Great Guildford Street
London
SE1 0ES
Tel: 0171 620 1111
Fax: 0171 261 9291
Campaigns against world poverty and seeks to identify and eliminate the causes of poverty.

INDEX

The Internet has been likened to shopping in a supermarket without aisles. The press of a button on a Web browser can bring up thousands of sites but working your way though them to find what you want can involve long and frustrating on-line searches. And unfortunately many sites contain inaccurate, misleading or heavily biased information. Our researchers have therefore undertaken an extensive analysis to bring you a selection of quality Web site addresses. If our readers feel that this new innovation in the series is useful, we plan to provide a more extensive Web site section in each new book in the *Issues* series.

* * * * *

AIDS Education and Research Trust (AVERT)
http://www.avert.org/talking.htm
Talking about Homosexuality in School
Reasons and recommendations for discussing homosexuality in secondary school. Questions which are often asked include whether people are born lesbian or gay, if it is a phase which one is going through, and what it means to 'come out'.
Facts are provided for teachers and other school staff. Information on HIV/AIDS and the causes and effects of homophobia are also discussed.
Summary: Useful advice on talking about same sex relationships in school. Based on a book by the same name.

Sharon Silverstein
silverst@cts.com
http://www.nyu.edu/pages/sls/gayworks
Details of legal recognition and protection of gay relationships. Slightly outdated (1995) information on same sex partnerships in Denmark, Sweden and Norway. Domestic partnership benefits are identified. The legalities of gay relationships in the United States are also covered.
Summary: Legal and nuptial rights for lesbian and gay partners.

Scriptural Biblical Perspective
http://209.75.2.6/support1.htm
An encouraging Biblical word of support for gay and lesbian Christians. This article points to scriptural passages related to gay sexuality, and argues that there is nothing incompatible with a gay/lesbian, Christian and loving, monogamous relationship.
Summary: Positive response to gay relationships from one Christian perspective.

Stonewall
http://www.Stonewall.org.uk
Provides background information on Stonewall along with recent press releases. A series of factsheets covers issues including gay sex and the law, public opinion, lesbian and gay parents, same sex couples and pension schemes, discrimination in the workplace etc.

Editor's note
Despite an extensive search we could not find any good quality Web sites which opposed homosexuality. The above selection may therefore appear weighted in favour of homosexuality. If any of our readers have found such a site, we would welcome inclusion of this information in a later edition.

ACKNOWLEDGEMENTS

The publisher is grateful for permission to reproduce the following material.

While every care has been taken to trace and acknowledge copyright, the publisher tenders its apology for any accidental infringement or where copyright has proved untraceable. The publisher would be pleased to come to a suitable arrangement in any such case with the rightful owner.

Chapter One: The Legal Aspects

Gay sex and the law, © Stonewall, *A global map of discrimination*, © War on Want, *Same sex couples and the law*, © Stonewall, January 1998, *Breaking the silence*, © Amnesty International, *Gays win sex at 16 battle*, © The Guardian, July 1997, *Discrimination in the workplace*, © Stonewall, January 1998, *Officials try to delay gays test case*, © The Guardian, January 1998, *Army's rethink over ban on gays*, © The Guardian, March 1997, *Pay ruling gives gays equal rights in Europe*, © The Guardian, October 1997, *Occupations*, © The Guardian / ICM Poll, *Gay civil Servants win pension rights for their partners*, © The Daily Mail, September 1997, *Lesbians and gay men at work*, © British Social Attitudes, *Playing it safe*, © Terrence Higgins Trust, June 1997.

Chapter Two: The Gay Debate

True colours, © Terrence Higgins Trust, 1997, *The social implications*, © The Maranatha Community, June 1997, *When a son breaks the news he is gay*, © The Independent, June 1997, *Gay rights have gone far enough*, © Leo McKinstry, July 1997, *Gay couples 'too few to be counted'*, © The Daily Mail, September 1996, *'The best option is to be open'*, © Telegraph Group Limited, London 1997, *The medical implications*, © The Maranatha Community, June 1997, *Disabled and homosexual*, © S.P.O.D., *Young gay men talking*, © AVERT, *Christianity and homosexuality*, © Lesbian & Gay Christian Movement, *Faith, hope and homosexuality*, © Evangelical Alliance, *Private lives*, © The Guardian, November 1997, *Synod decides to take a fresh look at old attitudes*, © The Independent, July 1997, *Gay pair insist on right to family child*, © The Guardian, May 1997, *Personal stories*, © Stonewall.

Photographs and illustrations:

Pages 1, 7, 9, 13, 17, 21, 23, 30, 31, 35, 36, 38: The Attic Publishing Co.

Thank you

Darin Jewell for assisting in the editorial research for this publication.

Craig Donnellan
Cambridge
April, 1998